MOSHE
DAYAN

MOSHE DAYAN

Richard Amdur

CHELSEA HOUSE PUBLISHERS
NEW YORK
PHILADELPHIA

Chelsea House Publishers
EDITOR-IN-CHIEF: Nancy Toff
EXECUTIVE EDITOR: Remmel T. Nunn
MANAGING EDITOR: Karyn Gullen Browne
COPY CHIEF: Juliann Barbato
PICTURE EDITOR: Adrian G. Allen
ART DIRECTOR: Maria Epes
MANUFACTURING MANAGER: Gerald Levine

World Leaders—Past & Present
SENIOR EDITOR: John W. Selfridge

Staff for MOSHE DAYAN
COPY EDITOR: Nicole Bowen
DEPUTY COPY CHIEF: Ellen Scordato
EDITORIAL ASSISTANT: Heather Lewis
PICTURE RESEARCHERS: Kathryn W. Bonomi and Leslie Seldin
ASSISTANT ART DIRECTOR: Laurie Jewell
DESIGNER: David Murray
PRODUCTION COORDINATOR: Joseph Romano
COVER ILLUSTRATION: Daniel O'Leary

First Printing

1 3 5 7 9 8 6 4 2

Library of Congress Cataloging-in-Publication Data

Amdur, Richard.
  Moshe Dayan / Richard Amdur.
  p.   cm.—(World leaders past & present)
  Bibliography: p.
  Includes index.
  ISBN 1-55546-829-2.
       0-7910-0673-5 (pbk.)
  1. Dayan, Moshe, 1915–1981—Juvenile literature.
2. Statesmen—Israel—Biography—Juvenile literature.
3. Generals—Israel—Biography—Juvenile literature.
4. Israel—Armed Forces—Biography—Juvenile literature.
I. Title. II. Series.
DS126.6.D3A83   1989
956.94′05′0924—dc19   88-32217
[B]   CIP

Contents

JOHN ADAMS

JOHN QUINCY ADAMS

KONRAD ADENAUER

ALEXANDER THE GREAT

SALVADOR ALLENDE

MARC ANTONY

CORAZON AQUINO

YASIR ARAFAT

KING ARTHUR

HAFEZ AL-ASSAD

KEMAL ATATÜRK

ATTILA

CLEMENT ATTLEE

AUGUSTUS CAESAR

MENACHEM BEGIN

DAVID BEN-GURION

OTTO VON BISMARCK

LÉON BLUM

SIMON BOLÍVAR

CESARE BORGIA

WILLY BRANDT

LEONID BREZHNEV

JULIUS CAESAR

JOHN CALVIN

JIMMY CARTER

FIDEL CASTRO

CATHERINE THE GREAT

CHARLEMAGNE

CHIANG KAI-SHEK

WINSTON CHURCHILL

GEORGES CLEMENCEAU

CLEOPATRA

CONSTANTINE THE GREAT

HERNÁN CORTÉS

OLIVER CROMWELL

GEORGES-JACQUES
   DANTON

JEFFERSON DAVIS

MOSHE DAYAN

CHARLES DE GAULLE

EAMON DE VALERA

EUGENE DEBS

DENG XIAOPING

BENJAMIN DISRAELI

ALEXANDER DUBČEK

FRANÇOIS & JEAN-CLAUDE
   DUVALIER

DWIGHT EISENHOWER

ELEANOR OF AQUITAINE

ELIZABETH I

FAISAL

FERDINAND & ISABELLA

FRANCISCO FRANCO

BENJAMIN FRANKLIN

FREDERICK THE GREAT

INDIRA GANDHI

MOHANDAS GANDHI

GIUSEPPE GARIBALDI

AMIN & BASHIR GEMAYEL

GENGHIS KHAN

WILLIAM GLADSTONE

MIKHAIL GORBACHEV

ULYSSES S. GRANT

ERNESTO "CHE" GUEVARA

TENZIN GYATSO

ALEXANDER HAMILTON

DAG HAMMARSKJÖLD

HENRY VIII

HENRY OF NAVARRE

PAUL VON HINDENBURG

HIROHITO

ADOLF HITLER

HO CHI MINH

KING HUSSEIN

IVAN THE TERRIBLE

ANDREW JACKSON

JAMES I

WOJCIECH JARUZELSKI

THOMAS JEFFERSON

JOAN OF ARC

POPE JOHN XXIII

POPE JOHN PAUL II

LYNDON JOHNSON

BENITO JUÁREZ

JOHN KENNEDY

ROBERT KENNEDY

JOMO KENYATTA

AYATOLLAH KHOMEINI

NIKITA KHRUSHCHEV

KIM IL SUNG

MARTIN LUTHER KING, JR.

HENRY KISSINGER

KUBLAI KHAN

LAFAYETTE

ROBERT E. LEE

VLADIMIR LENIN

ABRAHAM LINCOLN

DAVID LLOYD GEORGE

LOUIS XIV

MARTIN LUTHER

JUDAS MACCABEUS

JAMES MADISON

NELSON & WINNIE
   MANDELA

MAO ZEDONG

FERDINAND MARCOS

GEORGE MARSHALL

MARY, QUEEN OF SCOTS

TOMÁŠ MASARYK

GOLDA MEIR

KLEMENS VON METTERNICH

JAMES MONROE

HOSNI MUBARAK

ROBERT MUGABE

BENITO MUSSOLINI

NAPOLÉON BONAPARTE

GAMAL ABDEL NASSER

JAWAHARLAL NEHRU

NERO

NICHOLAS II

RICHARD NIXON

KWAME NKRUMAH

DANIEL ORTEGA

MOHAMMED REZA PAHLAVI

THOMAS PAINE

CHARLES STEWART
   PARNELL

PERICLES

JUAN PERÓN

PETER THE GREAT

POL POT

MUAMMAR EL-QADDAFI

RONALD REAGAN

CARDINAL RICHELIEU

MAXIMILIEN ROBESPIERRE

ELEANOR ROOSEVELT

FRANKLIN ROOSEVELT

THEODORE ROOSEVELT

ANWAR SADAT

HAILE SELASSIE

PRINCE SIHANOUK

JAN SMUTS

JOSEPH STALIN

SUKARNO

SUN YAT-SEN

TAMERLANE

MOTHER TERESA

MARGARET THATCHER

JOSIP BROZ TITO

TOUSSAINT L'OUVERTURE

LEON TROTSKY

PIERRE TRUDEAU

HARRY TRUMAN

QUEEN VICTORIA

LECH WALESA

GEORGE WASHINGTON

CHAIM WEIZMANN

WOODROW WILSON

XERXES

EMILIANO ZAPATA

ZHOU ENLAI

CHELSEA HOUSE PUBLISHERS

ON LEADERSHIP

Arthur M. Schlesinger, jr.

LEADERSHIP, it may be said, is really what makes the world go round. Love no doubt smooths the passage; but love is a private transaction between consenting adults. Leadership is a public transaction with history. The idea of leadership affirms the capacity of individuals to move, inspire, and mobilize masses of people so that they act together in pursuit of an end. Sometimes leadership serves good purposes, sometimes bad; but whether the end is benign or evil, great leaders are those men and women who leave their personal stamp on history.

Now, the very concept of leadership implies the proposition that individuals can make a difference. This proposition has never been universally accepted. From classical times to the present day, eminent thinkers have regarded individuals as no more than the agents and pawns of larger forces, whether the gods and goddesses of the ancient world or, in the modern era, race, class, nation, the dialectic, the will of the people, the spirit of the times, history itself. Against such forces, the individual dwindles into insignificance.

So contends the thesis of historical determinism. Tolstoy's great novel *War and Peace* offers a famous statement of the case. Why, Tolstoy asked, did millions of men in the Napoleonic Wars, denying their human feelings and their common sense, move back and forth across Europe slaughtering their fellows? "The war," Tolstoy answered, "was bound to happen simply because it was bound to happen." All prior history predetermined it. As for leaders, they, Tolstoy said, "are but the labels that serve to give a name to an end and, like labels, they have the least possible connection with the event." The greater the leader, "the more conspicuous the inevitability and the predestination of every act he commits." The leader, said Tolstoy, is "the slave of history."

Determinism takes many forms. Marxism is the determinism of class. Nazism the determinism of race. But the idea of men and women as the slaves of history runs athwart the deepest human instincts. Rigid determinism abolishes the idea of human freedom—

the assumption of free choice that underlies every move we make, every word we speak, every thought we think. It abolishes the idea of human responsibility, since it is manifestly unfair to reward or punish people for actions that are by definition beyond their control. No one can live consistently by any deterministic creed. The Marxist states prove this themselves by their extreme susceptibility to the cult of leadership.

More than that, history refutes the idea that individuals make no difference. In December 1931 a British politician crossing Park Avenue in New York City between 76th and 77th Streets around 10:30 P.M. looked in the wrong direction and was knocked down by an automobile—a moment, he later recalled, of a man aghast, a world aglare: "I do not understand why I was not broken like an eggshell or squashed like a gooseberry." Fourteen months later an American politician, sitting in an open car in Miami, Florida, was fired on by an assassin; the man beside him was hit. Those who believe that individuals make no difference to history might well ponder whether the next two decades would have been the same had Mario Constasino's car killed Winston Churchill in 1931 and Giuseppe Zangara's bullet killed Franklin Roosevelt in 1933. Suppose, in addition, that Adolf Hitler had been killed in the street fighting during the Munich *Putsch* of 1923 and that Lenin had died of typhus during World War I. What would the 20th century be like now?

For better or for worse, individuals do make a difference. "The notion that a people can run itself and its affairs anonymously," wrote the philosopher William James, "is now well known to be the silliest of absurdities. Mankind does nothing save through initiatives on the part of inventors, great or small, and imitation by the rest of us—these are the sole factors in human progress. Individuals of genius show the way, and set the patterns, which common people then adopt and follow."

Leadership, James suggests, means leadership in thought as well as in action. In the long run, leaders in thought may well make the greater difference to the world. But, as Woodrow Wilson once said, "Those only are leaders of men, in the general eye, who lead in action. . . . It is at their hands that new thought gets its translation into the crude language of deeds." Leaders in thought often invent in solitude and obscurity, leaving to later generations the tasks of imitation. Leaders in action—the leaders portrayed in this series—have to be effective in their own time.

And they cannot be effective by themselves. They must act in response to the rhythms of their age. Their genius must be adapted, in a phrase of William James's, "to the receptivities of the moment." Leaders are useless without followers. "There goes the mob," said the French politician hearing a clamor in the streets. "I am their leader. I must follow them." Great leaders turn the inchoate emotions of the mob to purposes of their own. They seize on the opportunities of their time, the hopes, fears, frustrations, crises, potentialities. They succeed when events have prepared the way for them, when the community is awaiting to be aroused, when they can provide the clarifying and organizing ideas. Leadership ignites the circuit between the individual and the mass and thereby alters history.

It may alter history for better or for worse. Leaders have been responsible for the most extravagant follies and most monstrous crimes that have beset suffering humanity. They have also been vital in such gains as humanity has made in individual freedom, religious and racial tolerance, social justice, and respect for human rights.

There is no sure way to tell in advance who is going to lead for good and who for evil. But a glance at the gallery of men and women in *World Leaders—Past and Present* suggests some useful tests.

One test is this: Do leaders lead by force or by persuasion? By command or by consent? Through most of history leadership was exercised by the divine right of authority. The duty of followers was to defer and to obey. "Theirs not to reason why / Theirs but to do and die." On occasion, as with the so-called enlightened despots of the 18th century in Europe, absolutist leadership was animated by humane purposes. More often, absolutism nourished the passion for domination, land, gold, and conquest and resulted in tyranny.

The great revolution of modern times has been the revolution of equality. The idea that all people should be equal in their legal condition has undermined the old structure of authority, hierarchy, and deference. The revolution of equality has had two contrary effects on the nature of leadership. For equality, as Alexis de Tocqueville pointed out in his great study *Democracy in America,* might mean equality in servitude as well as equality in freedom.

"I know of only two methods of establishing equality in the political world," Tocqueville wrote. "Rights must be given to every citizen, or none at all to anyone . . . save one, who is the master of all." There was no middle ground "between the sovereignty of all and the absolute power of one man." In his astonishing prediction of 20th-century totalitarian dictatorship, Tocqueville explained how the revolution of equality could lead to the *"Führerprinzip"* and more terrible absolutism than the world had ever known.

But when rights are given to every citizen and the sovereignty of all is established, the problem of leadership takes a new form, becomes more exacting than ever before. It is easy to issue commands and enforce them by the rope and the stake, the concentration camp and the *gulag.* It is much harder to use argument and achievement to overcome opposition and win consent. The Founding Fathers of the United States understood the difficulty. They believed that history had given them the opportunity to decide, as Alexander Hamilton wrote in the first Federalist Paper, whether men are indeed capable of basing government on "reflection and choice, or whether they are forever destined to depend . . . on accident and force."

Government by reflection and choice called for a new style of leadership and a new quality of followership. It required leaders to be responsive to popular concerns, and it required followers to be active and informed participants in the process. Democracy does not eliminate emotion from politics; sometimes it fosters demagoguery; but it is confident that, as the greatest of democratic leaders put it, you cannot fool all of the people all of the time. It measures leadership by results and retires those who overreach or falter or fail.

It is true that in the long run despots are measured by results too. But they can postpone the day of judgment, sometimes indefinitely, and in the meantime they can do infinite harm. It is also true that democracy is no guarantee of virtue and intelligence in government, for the voice of the people is not necessarily the voice of God. But democracy, by assuring the right of opposition, offers built-in resistance to the evils inherent in absolutism. As the theologian Reinhold Niebuhr summed it up, "Man's capacity for justice makes democracy possible, but man's inclination to injustice makes democracy necessary."

A second test for leadership is the end for which power is sought. When leaders have as their goal the supremacy of a master race or the promotion of totalitarian revolution or the acquisition and exploitation of colonies or the protection of greed and privilege or the preservation of personal power, it is likely that their leadership will do little to advance the cause of humanity. When their goal is the abolition of slavery, the liberation of women, the enlargement of opportunity for the poor and powerless, the extension of equal rights to racial minorities, the defense of the freedoms of expression and opposition, it is likely that their leadership will increase the sum of human liberty and welfare.

Leaders have done great harm to the world. They have also conferred great benefits. You will find both sorts in this series. Even "good" leaders must be regarded with a certain wariness. Leaders are not demigods; they put on their trousers one leg after another just like ordinary mortals. No leader is infallible, and every leader needs to be reminded of this at regular intervals. Irreverence irritates leaders but is their salvation. Unquestioning submission corrupts leaders and demeans followers. Making a cult of a leader is always a mistake. Fortunately hero worship generates its own antidote. "Every hero," said Emerson, "becomes a bore at last."

The signal benefit the great leaders confer is to embolden the rest of us to live according to our own best selves, to be active, insistent, and resolute in affirming our own sense of things. For great leaders attest to the reality of human freedom against the supposed inevitabilities of history. And they attest to the wisdom and power that may lie within the most unlikely of us, which is why Abraham Lincoln remains the supreme example of great leadership. A great leader, said Emerson, exhibits new possibilities to all humanity. "We feed on genius. . . . Great men exist that there may be greater men."

Great leaders, in short, justify themselves by emancipating and empowering their followers. So humanity struggles to master its destiny, remembering with Alexis de Tocqueville: "It is true that around every man a fatal circle is traced beyond which he cannot pass; but within the wide verge of that circle he is powerful and free; as it is with man, so with communities."

1

Common Cause

A young soldier climbed the stairs leading to the roof of a Lebanese police station. He and his platoon had just captured the building, killing or taking prisoner more than a dozen enemy troops in the process. The soldier clung desperately to his machine gun as the sound of gunfire continued to ring in his ears, the station still under siege by retreating forces who had taken cover in an adjacent orange grove.

Emerging from the stairwell the soldier saw that there was really nothing on the roof to shield him from enemy fire, only a short ledge. To take cover behind the ledge, however, he would have to crawl and then remain lying down, and this would not afford him an adequate view of the ground below.

Amidst the spray of bullets the soldier stood and opened random fire. Then, wanting to locate his aggressors, he raised to his eyes a pair of field glasses he had taken from a dead enemy soldier and trained them on his surroundings.

In 1941, Moshe Dayan fought alongside British troops against the Vichy French in Lebanon, then part of Syria. The Vichy regime, a Nazi collaborationist government, came to power in France following the German invasion of that country in 1940. Like many Jews, Dayan took up arms to stop Vichy troops from reaching Palestine.

It was early in the morning, June 8, 1941. World War II was nearly two years old, and the Germans — seeking world domination under the fascist leadership of dictator Adolf Hitler — were still on the offensive. Since the outbreak of war in September 1939, Germany had invaded and occupied Poland, Czechoslovakia, Austria, and France, and German bombs rained down on England as well. On June 1 of that year they had invaded the Soviet Union. Italy had entered the war on Germany's side.

In the Middle East, German and Italian forces were in a position of strength in the Libyan Desert to the west of Egypt, which was then a British colony. This threatened British control of the Suez Canal, the vital waterway linking the Mediterranean Sea with Asia. Britain also faced a challenge to the north, as Vichy French troops — soldiers of occupied France compelled to serve the Germans — were in Syria and on the move toward Palestine, which Britain had ruled since 1922.

In June 1941, as part of a general invasion of Syria, Britain sent a contingent of Australian soldiers into Lebanon — which was then a part of Syria — to destroy Vichy military installations there. Joining them were Jewish fighters who had volunteered to serve the British army in common cause against Germany. (Hitler, claiming that the Jews were responsible for all the world's ills, had instituted a "final solution" for their extermination — the establishment of death camps where they would be worked to death or simply killed outright.)

These Jewish soldiers came from the ranks of the Zionist settlers in Palestine, idealistic Jews who were trying to reestablish Jewish sovereignty in the Holy Land, from which their ancestors had been exiled some 2,000 years earlier. Hitler's anti-Semitic policies and murderous acts in Europe had prompted many Jews — those who could escape, at least — to make their way toward Palestine. Many other Jews from Europe, America, and elsewhere had been coming to Palestine since late in the 19th

Nazi soldiers jeer at a Jewish family in Memel, Germany, in the late 1930s. Hitler's anti-Semitic pronouncements convinced the German people that the Jews were to blame for Germany's depressed economy. His so-called final solution led to the extermination of 6 million Jews.

century, when the first stirrings of modern Zionism were heard. Thus, by the 1940s there was a generation of native-born Zionists in Palestine. Among them was that soldier dodging small-arms fire on the roof of a police station in Lebanon. His name was Moshe Dayan, who later wrote and spoke about what happened next:

> I had hardly got [the binoculars] into focus when a rifle bullet smashed into them, splintering a lens and the metal casing, which became embedded in the socket of my left eye. I immediately lost consciousness, but only for a moment. I came to and lay stretched out on my back. I was also wounded in the hand. . . . There was no chance to get to British forces for hours. I was lying on the roof bleeding, with a bullet and part of the field glasses in my head, and I thought that was the end. There was no doctor, no one even to attend to me, just a handkerchief over the bleeding eye socket. As I got weaker I began to lose consciousness and I thought, "You got a bullet in your head, and that's it. That's all there is."

Zalman Mart, the first man to reach the wounded Dayan, remembered what happened next: "I said, 'Moshe what do you think?' He's the kind of man you can talk to even when he's wounded. Moshe answered, 'I've lost the eye, but if I can reach a hospital in time, I'll live.' Now, how do you get to a hospital with the French shooting at you . . . and [there's] not a vehicle in sight?"

Dayan continues the story:

> I was then lowered in a makeshift stretcher of blankets to the ground floor, and there I lay, conscious all the time. Mart took my place on the machine gun but came down every so often to find out how I was doing and to report on what was happening. From then on, sightless, I followed the progress of the battle through my ears. . . . We had no pain killers with us, and my head felt as if it were being pounded with sledge hammers without stop. Fearing that I might not survive the loss of blood, one of the Australian officers suggested that I be handed over to the French so that I could receive medical treatment before it was too late. I refused.

General Moshe Dayan, Is-
raeli chief of staff, in 1954.
Dayan lost his left eye in
Syria in 1941, when his bin-
oculars were pierced by an
enemy bullet. The eye patch
he wore as a result became a
testament to his fearless dedication in battle.

Eighteen hours later, Dayan arrived at the Ha-
dassah Hospital in Jerusalem. Ruth Dayan later
wrote of her first sight of her wounded husband:
"When I was allowed to see him that night, his head
and both eyes were completely bandaged. The bridge
of the nose had been shattered and there were
countless fragments in Moshe's head. I noticed a
gaping hole near his nose where a tube had been
inserted so he could breathe. Another tube for
breathing was in his mouth. There were safety pins
in his nostrils to prevent choking. Both hands were
encased in enormous bandages, from which came
a horrible smell of fish oil. There was nothing that
I could do."

There was nothing Moshe could do, either, at least
at first. But he recovered and went on to wear his
scar of battle — a black eye-patch — proudly. Indeed,
both he and the patch would later come to symbolize
for the world the heroic modern Israeli — the daring,
charismatic soldier/citizen who triumphed over incredible odds, all the while maintaining a sense of
duty. The seeds of this character, planted first with
Dayan's ancestors in czarist Russia and then with
his settler parents in Palestine, had just borne fruit
in this early battle for the modern state of Israel.

2

The Making of a Soldier

Moshe Dayan was born on May 4, 1915, to Russian immigrant parents living in a small community known as Degania, an agricultural settlement founded in 1909 on the shores of the Jordan River and the Sea of Galilee in Palestine, as the Holy Land was then known. (The word Degania is a derivative of the Hebrew word for grain.) Dayan's parents had emigrated there because they were infused with a dream — to work the soil of the Holy Land with their hands, and, by so doing, work to reestablish Jewish sovereignty in the land their ancestors had been cast out of some 2,000 years before. That dream was shared by an increasing number of Jews in Europe and elsewhere and formed the basis of the Zionist movement.

Zionism came into being as a result of the Jews' longing to return to their ancient homeland and in response to anti-Semitism — prejudice against Jews — which had plagued the Jewish people for hundreds of years. Those Jews who came to Palestine around the turn of the century were following their dreams, fleeing from persecution, or both.

I set out to be a farmer—and I think I made quite a good farmer. Yet I have spent most of my adult life as a soldier, under arms.
—MOSHE DAYAN

Moshe Dayan, age six. The grandson of a rabbinical judge and the first child to be born on a *kibbutz*, or collective farm settlement, in Palestine, Moshe developed an early interest in Zionism, a movement that sought to establish a Jewish national community there.

History is rife with episodes of violence wrought against the Jews. The most memorable examples from ancient times were the destruction of two temples in Jerusalem. The first was built by King Solomon in the 10th century B.C. It became the center of Jewish religious worship and the symbol of an empire that stretched throughout ancient Palestine (which encompassed today's Israel and parts of Lebanon, Syria, Jordan, Iraq, and Egypt). The temple was razed by the Babylonians in 586 B.C. as part of their dynastic expansion; most of the Jews were taken to Babylonia to serve as slaves. In A.D. 66—70 the Romans destroyed a second temple built during a short-lived resurgence of Jewish power in the Holy Land. The Jews were sent into exile once again. Always, the Jews pledged to return some day to Jerusalem.

During the 14th and 15th centuries the Spanish Inquisition — an intensely violent campaign of religious intolerance — prompted the slaughter of Jews. The attack on the Jews during the Inquisition was also the result of jealousy: Many Jews had become financiers who were highly influential with the Spanish royal court and thus an easy target for a populace discontented with taxes or other economic hardships. Anti-Semitism, for similar reasons, existed throughout Germany, Poland, and Russia for centuries thereafter.

One episode of anti-Semitism in France rocked the country and became something of a bellwether for the Jews. In 1894 a Jewish army officer named Alfred Dreyfus was convicted of treason for passing important military information on to the Germans; he was condemned to life imprisonment on Devil's Island in French Guiana. In 1898 it was discovered that much of the evidence against Dreyfus had been forged. A year later he was pardoned, but it was not until 1906 that a court set aside the Dreyfus conviction as "wrongful" and "erroneous" and acknowledged its anti-Semitic roots. But by then the damage had been done. Exposure of anti-Semitism in France shocked the Jews because most of them had thought that France had been among the more enlightened and liberal countries in Europe. If such a thing could happen to us here, they thought, we are not safe anywhere.

Among the many people who reached this same conclusion was Theodor Herzl, the Paris correspondent of the Vienna *Neue Freie Presse* (New Free Press). Herzl covered the Dreyfus affair for the paper and witnessed mobs shouting "Death to the Jews"

An 1895 cover illustration from *Le Petit Journal*, a French newspaper, depicts Alfred Dreyfus, a Jewish captain in the French army, suffering public humiliation following his conviction on false treason charges. The Dreyfus affair was a national embarrassment for the French.

Theodor Herzl, Austrian playwright and Paris correspondent for the Vienna *Neue Freie Presse*, with his mother in his study. Perhaps more than any other individual, Herzl helped transform the vague ideals of many European Jews into the Zionist movement.

as part of the court proceedings. Herzl realized that the only way that the Jews could ever hope to live with dignity would be if they had a land of their own. He subsequently published a plan for immediate action aimed at securing a permanent Jewish state in the Jews' ancient homeland of Palestine, then populated with Arabs. The idea was not new, but Herzl's tireless work on behalf of it was. He captured the imagination of more and more Jews across Europe, among them Moshe Dayan's father, Shmuel, his uncle Eliyahu, and his grandfather.

Moshe's grandfather was a rabbinical judge (*dayan* in Hebrew), and consequently the family had easy access to a large collection of sacred books. Zionist periodicals also found their way into the family's hands, enabling them to read about a beautiful "land of milk and honey" and the pioneering efforts of the Jews to reclaim what was once theirs. Needless to say, this posed a marked contrast to the shabby Russian village in which the Dayans lived and the meager lives they led there.

In his autobiography, Dayan described his father's village, Zaskow, as "tumbledown." Still, the family was fortunate — they did not suffer from the persecution and pogroms (massacres) that were the lot of most Russian Jews. Thus were they able to cultivate their idealism and dream of joining the Zionists in Palestine, all the while saving their money to pay for the journey.

Eliyahu and Shmuel traveled to the Holy Land in 1908; four years later, Eliyahu, happy and satisfied as a farmer north of Tel Aviv, returned to Russia to retrieve his wife and children. Shmuel, meanwhile, became something of a journeyman farm laborer, working in Petach Tikvah, Rehovot, Ein Ganim, and Hadera, all towns and settlements bustling and growing with the activity of the increasing numbers of Jews who were arriving. Soon he was drawn to what was then the frontier — Galilee, in Palestine's north. As he wrote home after he had established himself in that part of the country, he was proud to have become "a laborer in Galilee, with a *kefieh* [Arab headdress], riding boots, a pistol at my hip, and mule reins in my hand."

Palestine at the time was ruled by the Ottoman Turks as part of an empire that at its height in the 18th century stretched from Persia in the east to central Europe in the west and north and to Egypt in the south. By the 20th century, however, the Ottomans had been in decline for many years. Chaim Weizmann, who succeeded Herzl as the Zionist movement's leader, wrote in his memoirs, *Trial and Error*, that Palestine was "one of the most neglected corners of the miserably neglected Turkish Empire."

More distressing for the Jews than the malaria, typhus, and oppressive heat was that in a land they were calling their own the Jews were outnumbered by nearly 10 to 1. Of a total population of some 600,000, only about 60,000 were Jews, with Muslims numbering about half a million and Christians the rest. Though the Second Aliyah had been under way since 1904, many more Jews would be needed if the Zionists were to make any impression on the landscape. (The word *Aliyah*, Hebrew for *ascent*, is the term given to the process of immigrating to the Holy Land.) What settlements there were were poorly run, kept afloat by money from abroad.

Still, the Turks were wary of the increased numbers of Jews in the country. Most of the newcomers were involved in business or commerce with foreign powers that, the Turks feared, could interfere in the administration of their empire. The local Arab population, too, was alarmed by the prospect of Jewish statehood. They felt that the Jews would rob them of their livelihood and banish them from their land.

Shmuel, a Zionist since the age of 15, was not deterred by these conditions. Indeed, displaying mettle and conviction, in 1911 he joined Degania. Three years later he married Dvorah, another Russian immigrant, who had reached Degania through a contact of her father's. It was an unlikely match. Shmuel was thoroughly invested with the Zionist ideal and actively involved in movement politics. Dvorah had had a secular Russian upbringing and had worked for many years on behalf of the needy before being exposed to Zionism. Once she became acquainted with Zionism, though, she was immediately taken with a newfound desire to explore her Jewish identity. It was not long before she decided to leave for Palestine. Her application to Degania was rejected at first — Dvorah was small in size and somewhat frail, and the community's members thought she might not be strong enough for the rigors of agricultural life. They also questioned her zeal. Dvorah proved them wrong on both counts.

On May 4, 1915, Dvorah gave birth to Moshe, naming him after another member of Degania who had been killed a year earlier by Arab robbers. Moshe's birth was significant in another way — not only was he the first child born at Degania, he was the first child born to the unique social experiment being pioneered by the Degania Zionists, the *kibbutz*.

The kibbutz was a communal, or collective, settlement based on complete equality among its members in work, housing, education, and nearly all other aspects of life. This type of living arrangement grew out of a search for an effective and efficient way to settle and farm land in Palestine and a desire for new colonies in remote and border areas of the country. The idea of the kibbutz emerged from the utopian ideas of Zionist settlers, who were often interested in and influenced by the writings of Russian socialists and communists.

Kibbutzim (*im* is the plural suffix in Hebrew) are built on land owned by the Jewish National Fund.

In most cases, one main building serves as the place where relatively large numbers congregate — dining hall, meeting hall, theater. Education, medical services, and other necessities are provided by qualified kibbutz members or by individuals from other kibbutzim. (Kibbutzim are part of a larger framework known as the kibbutz movement; there are some doctrinal differences within this movement.) Kibbutz residents, or kibbutzniks, contribute according to their abilities and receive according to their needs. The welfare of the community is paramount; individual desires are often suppressed for this perceived greater good.

The kibbutz movement was in the vanguard of Jewish settlement of Palestine. Indeed, some early kibbutzniks dreamed that the state of Israel would be one large kibbutz. That has not happened, but kibbutzniks have had an influence on the development of Israel well out of proportion to their numbers. Though constituting roughly three percent of Israel's population, kibbutzniks can be found in leading roles in the military, in government, and throughout Israeli society.

Moshe's infancy and childhood years were marked by important changes in the physical and political landscape of Palestine. World War I, which lasted from 1914 to 1918, led to the complete dissolution of the Ottoman Empire, as British and French forces drove the Turks out of the region. Great Britain later assumed control of Palestine, being granted a mandate there by the League of Nations (which was later replaced by the United Nations). Just prior to its military success in Palestine, Britain issued the Balfour Declaration, which read as follows:

> His Majesty's Government view with favor the establishment in Palestine of a national home for the Jewish people and will use their best endeavors to facilitate the achievement of that object, it being clearly understood that nothing shall be done which may prejudice the civil and religious rights and political rights of existing non-Jewish communities in Palestine, or the rights and political status enjoyed by Jews in any other country.

The mayor of Jerusalem (holding a cane) surrenders the city to British troops. On December 9, 1917, Jerusalem fell to the British, ending 400 years of Ottoman Turkish rule over the holy city.

The statement is considered to have been the first major governmental action legitimizing the Jewish quest for a homeland. Suddenly, the language of idealistic settlers had become the language of one of the world's most powerful governments.

Changes occurred in the Dayan household as well. Shmuel found himself frequently at odds with the inhabitants of Degania on a variety of issues. For one thing, he felt uncomfortable with what he saw as the feeling of many Degania residents that they could rest easy after having launched and established a successful kibbutz. Shmuel believed that a new conquest was called for and so helped to found a separate community nearby. On a more fundamental level, Shmuel was tiring of the intense collectivism that was the dominant feature of the kibbutz. He felt that there had to be a better way to serve both the needs of the budding nation and those of the individual. This personal crisis led to a severe deterioration in Shmuel's relations with his cosettlers. Indeed, Shabtai Teveth, one of Moshe Dayan's biographers, wrote that Shmuel was mostly remembered as "stubborn, cantankerous, egoistic, ambitious, and often insincere."

In the late 19th and early 20th centuries Jewish settlers in Palestine were challenged not only by the usual rigors of agricultural life but also by oppressive heat and a scarcity of water. Outbreaks of malaria and typhoid also tested the mettle of the Zionist pioneers.

Wheat harvesting on the first *moshav*, called Nahalal, in southeastern Israel near the Gaza Strip. In 1921 the Dayans and other Zionists who were disenchanted with the intense collectivization of the kibbutzim founded Nahalal, a semicommunal settlement allowing private land ownership.

Thus the Dayans decided to leave Degania and join other Zionists of similar ideology in founding Nahalal, the first *moshav*. A moshav differs from a kibbutz in that it is made up of individual farmers who own their own land and live in their own homes but choose to collectivize other aspects of their lives. They may share farming equipment, for example, or educate their children collectively.

Nahalal prospered and grew, eventually becoming the prototype for the hundreds of moshavim that now exist in Israel. Moshe described the settlement in his 1976 autobiography: "The layout was like a giant cartwheel, with the communal buildings at the hub, the farmers' cottages forming an inner circle, and their plots of land radiating out to the perimeter like the spokes of the wheel. Ours was one of eight homesteads, with each family cultivating 20 acres. Some of the farm facilities were jointly owned, while both the marketing of the produce and the purchase of supplies were done through cooperative channels. Some of the basic tenets of the kibbutz were preserved — the ideological importance of tilling the soil, of working with one's own hands, and of complete equality of the members."

Moshe's life on Nahalal naturally involved farming chores — milking, plowing, planting, and reaping —

Haganah members service their firearms. The primary security force for the Jews of Palestine, the Haganah adhered to a policy of restraint, taking action only in response to violent attacks on Jews or their property. Dayan joined the group in 1929.

as well as domestic work such as kneading dough for bread and stirring the tub of fig jam his mother made. In the moshav school, Moshe excelled in writing and drawing and in his nature and Bible studies. His classmates remember him as having a strong personality. One in particular recalled "the Dayan trait of haughtiness, contempt for others. . . . His very attitude provoked opposition." Another said that Moshe was "uncompromisingly aggressive. If he fought a boy, it was not enough merely to beat him. If there was mud on the ground . . . he wouldn't rest until he had plastered the boy's face with it."

In 1927, Moshe and the other boys of Nahalal began to share guard duty with their parents. Their primary assignment was to make sure that local Arabs' herds did not graze on moshav lands. This type of work apparently appealed to Moshe, for in 1929 he joined the Haganah.

The Haganah (Hebrew for *defense*) was the primary security force for the Jews of Palestine. Formed as the Turks left — and more and more Jews entered — the country following World War I, the Haganah followed a general policy of *havlagah*, or restraint, which meant that it was a defensive force to be used only if Jews or their property were attacked. The need for such an organization became especially important following Arab rioting in 1929 in Hebron, Jerusalem, Haifa, and elsewhere that left more than 125 Jews dead and hundreds more wounded. Movement leaders felt that it had become necessary for every able-bodied Jewish youth to enroll. However, membership in the organization and the bearing of arms were deemed illegal by the British.

In 1934, Ruth Shwarz, the daughter of a prominent Jerusalem lawyer, arrived at Nahalal to attend the agricultural school there, which had been started a few years earlier by the World International Zionist Organization. She and Moshe, also a student, became friends very quickly. Ruth, another *sabra*, or native-born Jew, had lived with her family in London, where she learned to speak English. She gave Moshe lessons as they walked the grounds of Nahalal. On July 12, 1935, the two were married.

According to Teveth, the marriage of Moshe and Ruth was "a society match between children of prominent members of the Second Aliyah intelligentsia and the communal settlement on the one hand, and the political, English-speaking elite, on the other." Among the guests at the lavish affair were Dr. Arthur Ruppin, an important supporter of Jewish farm settlement in Palestine; Moshe Sharett, who later became prime minister; Dov Hos, one of the leaders of the Jewish Agency; and the entire Arab el-Mazarib tribe. (Moshe and a number of Nahalal residents had many friends among the Arabs.) The only people who stayed away were those of Ruth's friends who were upset with her for forsaking the kibbutz movement — she had come to Nahalal as part of her prekibbutz training — for life on a moshav.

Moshe and Ruth left for what was to be an extended stay in London. They were to have a honeymoon, and Moshe was then to study agriculture at Cambridge University. But in early 1936 the newlyweds were summoned back to Palestine — Moshe was needed by the Haganah, as the Jews found themselves in the midst of another round of hostilities with the Arabs.

In April 1936 an organized uprising commonly known as the Arab Revolt erupted. The culmination of months of tension, the violence was particularly

The city of Jerusalem. Throughout its history from ancient times to the present, Jerusalem has been a coveted prize for generations of conquerors and has been captured, surrendered, and recaptured repeatedly by various warring peoples.

Haganah leaders Dayan, Yigal Allon (left and right with rifles), and Yitzhak Sadeh (center). In 1938, the group established Kibbutz Hanita, but Dayan, an individualist like his father, found the communal life of the kibbutz limiting, and he and his wife Ruth stayed there only a few months.

strong in 1936 and continued sporadically for the next several years.

Britain, acting to restore order, ferried in extra troops from Egypt, Malta, and England. Next, a commission, headed by Lord William Robert Wellesley Peel, was formed to investigate the situation and make recommendations. (In 1937 the panel floated a novel, startling idea that no one had yet considered in any detail — dividing the disputed territories into two separate, independent states. This came to be known as partition.) Finally, the British established the Supernumerary Police, a Jewish-manned force that would operate under the command of the British.

Dayan joined this force and by 1938 had become an instructor. He also served as a field guide, helping the British navigate the terrain and landscape around an important oil pipeline from Iraq that was considered one of the "lifelines" of the entire British Empire and that was repeatedly subject to Arab sabotage. At the same time, Dayan was made a platoon leader in the Haganah. He and another new platoon leader, Yigal Allon, were quickly given the chance to prove themselves.

Jewish leaders in Palestine, sensing that partition of the land would sooner or later be the basis for negotiated peace, had decided that more settlements were needed — especially in the north — as a way of "securing" territory for the state-to-be. In March 1938, in the largest operation it had yet undertaken, the Haganah, led by Dayan and Allon, founded Kibbutz Hanita near the Lebanese border. They used the common, so-called tower and fence system: By dark of night, Jewish forces reached a chosen site, quickly erected a watchtower, perimeter fence, and tents, and then defended it all against the furious Arab artillery and gun barrage that greeted them at daybreak. Such a "fact on the ground" (as Dayan would later call these settlements), once in place, was hard to erase. Dayan and his wife stayed at Hanita for several months, but Moshe soon found that, like his father, he was too much of an individualist for the communal life of a kibbutz.

While at Hanita, Dayan met a British soldier and intelligence officer who would have a formative influence on him. As another Hanita resident recalled, "One night a taxi came to Hanita and an extraordinary figure stepped out. He carried two rifles, a dictionary, and some Hebrew newspapers. We gazed at him in amazement. His daring at coming up to Hanita alone at night astonished us and made a tremendous impression." This was Scottish artillery captain Orde Charles Wingate, who was sent by the British to help quell the Arab riots and to protect British interests in Palestine.

Wingate, a strong supporter of the Zionist cause, used the men of the Haganah for special nighttime operations. These missions helped both the British and the Jews, as the Haganah learned top-notch military skills from Wingate. Dayan wrote, "I was greatly impressed. . . . There was a professionalism about Wingate, a positiveness, a stubborn lack of compromise. A dominating personality, he infected us all with his fanaticism and faith."

Eventually, however, Wingate's Zionist sympathies proved too much for the British, who were becoming less and less sympathetic to the Jewish cause. Wingate was recalled to London and later died in Burma during World War II.

World War II took center stage for the Jews as well. With the rise of Adolf Hitler as head of Germany's Nazi party, the establishment of the Jewish homeland became a matter of survival. Hitler came to power by portraying himself as a powerful leader devoted to the German "fatherland." The image appealed to many Germans in part because of their country's devastating loss in World War I and because of crushing economic difficulties at home. Hitler also advanced racial policies, declaring the Aryan Germans to be a pure, superior race destined to rule the world. The Jews, he claimed, were responsible for all of society's ills and therefore had to be destroyed. Thus, the Jews of Germany faced constant harassment and humiliation. They were discriminated against in terms of jobs, housing, and education and were beaten, boycotted, and forced to live in ghettos. Such appalling policies and prac-

During his brief stay at Hanita, Dayan met Scottish artillery captain Orde Charles Wingate, who was sent there to look after British interests in Palestine. Wingate impressed the young soldiers with his keen military mind, and some of his stubbornness rubbed off on Dayan.

Two prisoners in a Nazi concentration camp. The goal of Hitler's final solution was the complete annihilation of the Jewish race. Millions of Jews were rounded up and sent to concentration camps, where they were usually used as slaves and then either shot or gassed.

tices were sanctioned by the German government with the passage of the Nuremberg Laws of 1935.

Hitler's rise led to a near doubling of the Jewish presence in Palestine as Jews emigrated to flee the Nazis. By 1939 the Jewish population in Palestine had grown to nearly 500,000. But Palestinian Arabs, who still outnumbered Palestinian Jews, were by then calling for an Arab state in Palestine. They had seen the other Arab states — Syria, Transjordan, and Iraq — move toward independence and autonomy, and wanted the same for themselves. Also the Arabs feared that the rapidly increasing Jewish immigrant population would make them a minority in their own land. As these two nationalisms, Jewish and Arab, continued to compete over the same tiny sliver of land, Palestine was becoming a tinderbox.

On September 29, 1938, the English prime minister Arthur Neville Chamberlain, in the face of an increasingly aggressive German regime, signed the Munich Pact with Adolf Hitler. The Germans had occupied Austria and parts of Czechoslovakia earlier in the year. The Munich Pact was supposed to put a stop to German belligerence; it committed Germany to ceasing its hostility toward Czechoslovakia

in exchange for its assuming control of the Sude-
tenland, a region of that country with a large German population. However, hardly a soul believed
that Germany would abide by the pact's terms — its
appetite for territory and power was too large. Indeed, the agreement only served to fortify German
ambitions and contribute to the outbreak of war.

The agreement was roundly denounced on its
signing and stands today as the epitome of national
weakness. As several English papers said at the
time, "In Munich honor died." Jewish leaders feared
that a similar British cave-in could happen in Palestine in the face of a strong Arab front.

Chamberlain's foreign secretary, Anthony Eden,
resigned in protest, but he left a legacy that also
dashed Zionist hopes. Eden had decided earlier in
the year to abandon the concept of partition and
instead court the Arabs. He planned to have ibn-
Saud, a leading Arab nationalist and the head of
the Kingdom of Saudi Arabia, rule the entire region

under British aegis. Eden appointed a commission, this one chaired by Sir John Woodhead, to examine the concept of partition. (Zionists christened this the Re-Peel Commission.) Its report, released on November 9, 1938, stated that the partition of the Holy Land was "impracticable" and offered a "best-case" scenario — a Jewish state of some 400 square miles along Palestine's coastal plain.

That night, as the Jews reeled from this blow, German Jews suffered through something worse — the infamous Kristallnacht (Crystal Night). Hitler's storm troopers, in a night of rampage and depredation, destroyed and burned homes, synagogues, and shops owned by Jews and beat and arrested vast numbers of people. Known as Kristallnacht because of the countless fragments of shattered glass, it marked the beginning of Hitler's "final solution" to the "Jewish problem."

As war looked more and more certain, the British became fearful that the Arabs might align themselves with Germany to achieve their aims in Palestine (as they had fought alongside the British during World War I to throw off the Ottoman Empire). In an attempt to stave off this possibility, and as a way of further currying favor with the Arabs, in 1939 Britain issued a document called the white paper, which decreed that Jewish immigration in Palestine would end following the admission of 75,000 immigrants during the next five years, thus forever keeping the Jews a minority in Palestine. The white paper also sought to limit Jewish purchases of Arab land and said that British policy did not back the establishment of a Jewish state in Palestine. Expressing the Zionists' outrage, Chaim Weizmann referred to the white paper as a "death sentence," while Arab leaders, distrustful of the British, also rejected the document.

In late August 1939, the Soviet Union and Germany, both of which coveted Poland, announced that they had reached a nonaggression pact. Far from signifying a lessening of hostilities, the treaty instead set the stage for war. Sure enough, on September 1, Nazi bombs rained down on Warsaw. Two days later France and Great Britain declared war on Germany.

World War II sparked a total upheaval for the lives of people from Europe to the Orient. For the Jews of Europe it meant genocide. Under the direction of Hitler's Nazis, Jews were shipped to death camps, where they were either killed outright or first used as slaves and then murdered. In the next few years, millions of Jews died in the camps — but only after the Nazis had taken their jewelry, gold teeth, and clothes.

In Palestine, meanwhile, the British began to crack down on the activities of the Jews and, in particular, of the Haganah. In September 1939, Dayan and a group of 42 other men were arrested and subsequently sentenced to five years' imprisonment in the famed Crusader fortress at Acre. The Yishuv, the Jewish community in Palestine, was shocked at the turn of events and sentiments.

"We are beginning to feel how prison life slowly replaces our previous way of life," wrote Dayan from Acre to Ruth and his baby daughter, Yael, born earlier in the year. "Everything in our past is turning into memories. Our thoughts revolve upon the sandwiches we get here, and the content of our lives is growing impoverished and wretched."

As the months wore on, Dayan took a more philosophic view of his plight: "When it's over, I'll go out, have a good wash and start life anew. Acre is no rest home but it isn't a medieval dungeon either, nor Siberia. This is part of the struggle for a state, and I'm sorry we are in jail as a result of a luckless error [being caught] and not of some special operation with significant impact. What is particularly burdensome for all of us is being cooped up and helpless while a war in which we all desperately wish to take part is being waged."

It took the presence of German forces in Syria for Britain to change its policy toward the Jews. Worried that the Germans might be well on their way to invading and occupying Palestine, the British realized they could use the help of the Jewish fighters. In February 1941 the British released Dayan and his 42 comrades. Three months later the British called Dayan into action on their behalf. The result of that mission was the black eye-patch for which he became known.

Dayan at the Crusader fortress at Acre, where he was imprisoned in 1939. Dayan and more than 40 others were arrested that September for taking part in anti-British activities following the issuance of the 1939 white paper.

3

The War of Independence

During World War II both the Jews and Arabs observed a relative truce with the British, who were consumed by the effort, in alliance with the United States, France, and others, to defeat the Axis powers of Germany and Italy. Cooperation with the British put the Zionists in a particularly difficult situation, however. On the one hand, the British were fighting against the Hitler menace, to the obvious benefit of Jews and non-Jews everywhere. Accordingly, more than 30,000 Palestinian Jews joined the Allied armies. On the other hand, Britain repeatedly refused to ease its immigration policies regarding Palestine, turning a cold shoulder on desperate European Jews for whom escape to Palestine was a matter of survival. This apparent indifference to the fate of the Jews, coupled with the British repudiation of the Balfour Declaration, further infuriated the Zionists.

> *There is no other way apart from a war of liberation.*
> —MENACHEM BEGIN
> as leader of the Irgun

The S.S. *Exodus* was carrying nearly 5,000 Jewish refugees when it was seized by British naval units. Adhering to policies outlined in the 1939 white paper, the British denied thousands of homeless Jews entry into Palestine, often by seizing shiploads of illegal immigrants.

—proclamation of the Irgun Zvei Leumi, declaring rebellion against British occupation, 1943

Though the British and the other Allies were reluctant to admit it, and despite the British invasion of Syria, the prospects for a German takeover of Palestine seemed very good. The British decided to prepare for this possibility by, among other things, installing a series of radio communications facilities that could be used for spying operations behind enemy lines. Dayan, again cooperating with the British and working out of a home base in Jerusalem, created what became known as Moshe Dayan's network.

But then, in October 1942, German and Italian forces were defeated at the Battle of El Alamein in Egypt by Allied troops under the command of Britain's general Bernard Montgomery. It was a turning point in the war, marking the beginning of the end of German domination of North Africa and removing the immediate Axis threat to the Middle East.

As an Allied victory in the war became more apparent over the course of the following year, some Zionist leaders in Palestine felt that the need for restraint toward the British had diminished. Some Jews took up arms against them.

The Irgun Z'vai Leumi (National Military Organization) strongly disagreed with the Haganah's defensive character and believed instead in an aggressive approach to the British and the Arabs. The Irgun advocated active opposition to British rule in Palestine, although they agreed, at least initially, to cease anti-British activities during the war. The Irgun's philosophy of armed power and displays of force was condemned by the Jewish Agency and most of the Yishuv. A particular point of disagreement was that the Irgun did not help establish such necessary institutions as settlements, hospitals, and service agencies for the future Jewish state but concentrated mainly on waging war. An offshoot of the Irgun, the Lohomei Herut Israel (Fighters for the Freedom of Israel), known by the Hebrew acronym of Lehi and to English speakers as the Stern gang (after Avraham Stern, the group's founder), took the Irgun policies to an extreme, often dealing in terrorism and political assassination.

In early 1944 the Irgun's leader, Menachem Begin, declared "war" on the British; over the next several months its 600 fighters bombed immigration, tax, and police offices in Jerusalem, Tel Aviv, and Haifa, stole arms from a British camp, and even stole money from fellow Jews in order to fund their campaign. Both the Irgun and the British suffered casualties along the way. The British deported captured Irgun and Lehi fighters to East Africa and placed a reward on Begin's head.

The Irgun also incurred the wrath of the Zionist establishment, who called them "maniacs, bandits, and nihilists" who "stabbed Zionism in the back." So rancorous were these intra-Zionist feelings that, at times, it appeared as if civil war among the Jews was a distinct possibility.

On November 6, 1944, Lord Walter Edward Guinness Moyne, England's minister for Middle East affairs and a close friend of English prime minister Winston Churchill, was assassinated in Cairo by two young Lehi members. The killing stunned the Jews, the British, and the world at large.

Haaretz, the influential Jewish newspaper in Palestine, published an article in which it was claimed, "Since Zionism began, no more grievous blow has been struck at our cause."

Churchill, speaking bluntly to the English House of Commons, said, "A shameful crime has shocked the world and affected none more strongly than those like myself who, in the past, have been consistent friends of the Jews and constant architects of their future. If our dreams for Zionism are to end in the smoke of assassins' pistols, and one labors for its future to produce only a new set of gangsters worthy of Nazi Germany, many like myself would have to reconsider the position we have maintained so consistently and so long in the past."

The Jewish Agency issued a statement saying that "the Yishuv is required to spew up all members of this destructive and ruinous gang, to deny them shelter and refuge, not to give into their threats and to grant the authorities all the aid required to prevent the acts of terror and liquidate its organization,

In 1944, Menachem Begin, leader of the radical underground resistance group called the Irgun, launched a terrorist campaign against the British in Palestine. The group's violent tactics were condemned by Zionists, and the Haganah arrested many Irgun members.

for our lives depend on it."

What became known as the hunting season began. Its goal was to destroy the Irgun. The Haganah arrested Irgunists throughout Palestine and gave names of Irgunists and their supporters to the British authorities. For seven months the tyranny continued, but ultimately the Jewish Agency came to view the Moyne assassination as a "bitter and tragic necessity." For their cooperation with the British the Jewish Agency received no reward — no relaxation in immigration laws and no further support for a homeland. Worse, the fratricidal atmosphere of the hunting season left scars on all involved and worsened an already bad situation.

The spring and summer of 1945 brought the end of World War II: In May, Germany surrendered unconditionally, and by the end of August, Japan, devastated by the atomic bombs dropped on its cities by the United States, came to heel as well. Also that summer, Winston Churchill stepped down after a Labour party victory in the British election. The Labour party had promised to rescind the white paper and work for the creation of a Jewish state in Palestine, so when Labour won the election the Zionists rejoiced.

The new Labour government of Prime Minister Clement Atlee and Foreign Secretary Ernest Bevin wasted little time in making a veritable mockery of the central tenets of Zionism. First, the British allowed a monthly immigration quota of only 1,500, when thousands could have poured in almost daily. Second, Bevin tried to argue that the Jewish survivors of the Holocaust still had a future in Europe. Bevin's apparent ignorance as to the seriousness of the Jewish plight was confirmed by numerous public statements Bevin went on to make in which he clumsily trampled on Jewish sensitivities.

The Jews attempted to bring Jews into Palestine illegally, and the British responded by refusing to allow ships carrying illegal Jewish immigrants entry to Palestine. In one instance several ships, carrying thousands of European refugees who had managed to reach Romanian and Turkish ports, were turned away from the shores of Palestine by British au-

thorities. Some of the refugees were sent back where they had come from; others were placed in internment camps on the island of Cyprus, south of Turkey. One group of Jews blew up their ship, the S.S. *Patria*, rather than comply with an order by the British high commission for Palestine to sail for the island of Mauritius in the Indian Ocean. More than 250 men, women, and children drowned as a result of this act of defiance.

Another ship, the S.S. *Struma*, carrying more than 750 people on a vessel normally suited for about 100, sank off the coast of Istanbul after months in immigration limbo.

David Ben-Gurion, the leader of the Yishuv, stated that "the acts of the British government are a continuation of Hitler's policy of hostility." He then did the unthinkable — he turned to the Irgun and Lehi and asked them to join the Haganah in forming a united resistance movement. Ben-Gurion had no illusions that the relatively small coalition could drive the British out. He discouraged the use of violent means toward political ends, but he felt that armed resistance against the British was the only course of action left. He also thought that the resistance would provoke a British counterattack that would draw world attention to, and perhaps create sympathy for, the Zionist cause.

Jewish refugees who were denied entry into Palestine were usually sent back to their port of departure. Many, however, were placed in internment camps such as this one on the island of Cyprus, south of Turkey.

The three groups agreed to act in close concert with one another — but not to merge their forces. The coalition, called the Hebrew Resistance Movement, swung into action in the autumn of 1945 with terrorist attacks on railway installations and British police targets. The groups also raided British stores of arms, destroyed planes belonging to the Royal Air Force, and blew up major bridges connecting Palestine to its neighbors. By mid-1946, Palestine had become an armed camp, complete with bunkers, sandbags, motorized patrols, and 100,000 British soldiers and policemen. Yet the resistance, made up of just 5,000 fighters, held the British in check. As J. Bowyer Bell wrote in *Terror Out of Zion*, "The mandate became a garrison state under internal siege, and the garrison [military installation], despite its size, equipment, and determination, proved ineffectual and self-defeating."

On Saturday, June 29, the British began their most forceful and effective response — an operation that came to be known as Black Sabbath. Nearly 3,000 Jews were detained, among them some of the movement's leaders, and a curfew was put in place. British soldiers swooped down on Tel Aviv, searching block by block and house to house for arms and for resistance fighters in hiding. The Irgun responded with the most violent attack ever aimed at the British in Palestine.

The British nerve center in Palestine, the headquarters of their administration, was the King David Hotel in Jerusalem, a luxury establishment overlooking the Old City. On July 22, 1946, 350 kilograms of dynamite exploded in the hotel, demolishing much of it and killing 91 people: 28 Britons, 41 Arabs, 17 Jews, 2 Armenians, 1 Russian, 1 Greek, and 1 Egyptian. The operation, planned as a symbolic attack on British prestige, but not one that would claim so many casualties, has been called a "tragedy of errors." The attack received international condemnation and remains one of the most controversial incidents in Israel's history.

The bombing spelled the end of the united resistance movement. The Haganah issued a public statement saying, "The Hebrew Resistance Movement denounces the heavy toll of lives caused in the dissidents' operation at the King David Hotel" and returned to its old view of the Irgun as a renegade band of terrorists.

The operation at least partly achieved its desired objective: Britain began to wonder if its presence in Palestine was more trouble than it was worth.

Dayan spent much of this turbulent time at Nahalal recovering from his injury. At first he had been very depressed by what had happened. As he commented, "As far as the Haganah was concerned, I was an invalid, unfit for action. Personally, I too felt that I was no longer capable of military activities of any kind, and all I was good for now was work as a night watchman or something like that. It became painfully clear to me that physically I was finished, incapable of anything connected with fighting." Such uncharacteristically gloomy comments from Dayan were testimony to the devastation he felt at the loss of his eye. Indeed, it wasn't until 1948 that he again became embroiled in the military struggle for independence.

Dayan focused instead on his settled, domestic life at Nahalal. In 1942 his first son, Ehud, was born; "Udi" was followed in 1945 by another boy,

The Dayan family (left to right) — Ruth, Assaf, Moshe, Ehud, and Yael — in 1950.

Assaf. As Yael recalled in her book, *My Father, His Daughter*, "Both my parents, on various occasions, referred to the years following our return to Nahalal as their happiest. These were the years between the two wars [World War II and the Arab-Israeli war]. The one had destroyed our people, and the other secured our national home. If this was happiness on borrowed time, my parents didn't realize it, and as far as they knew or planned, life was going to consist of making the cows produce more milk, fighting insects and worms that bugged the cauliflower, and harvesting a better yield of wheat. Hopes had to do with rainfall, farm machinery, and a new coop for the chickens, and disasters meant drought, a cow giving birth to a dead calf, or a foot-and-mouth cattle epidemic, which hurt our farm badly. . . . My father's involvement with public, military, or political affairs was minimal."

In the spring of 1947, Britain pronounced its mandate in Palestine "unworkable," sought United Nations help in finding a political solution, and announced its intention to withdraw from Palestine. In November the United Nations General Assembly voted to partition Palestine into a Jewish state and an Arab state. According to Israeli journalist Amos Elon, "The basic premise underlying the decision was that two intense nationalisms had clashed over Palestine. Both possessed validity and yet were totally irreconcilable. Regardless of the historical origins of the conflict, the rights and wrongs of the promises and counterpromises, the basic fact was the presence in the country of 650,000 Jews and 1,220,000 Arabs."

Weizmann, Ben-Gurion, and the mainstream Zionists reluctantly supported the partition plan. They reasoned that even a partitioned homeland was preferable to continued uncertainty and violence. Said one Zionist spokesperson, "This sacrifice would be the Jewish contribution to the solution of a painful problem and would bear witness to the Jewish people's spirit of international cooperation and its desire for peace."

The Arabs objected to the partition plan for several reasons: They believed that Palestine was theirs and

had been for years, and they resented a settlement being forced upon them. Why did European guilt over the treatment of the Jews in World War II have to be soothed in the Middle East? they asked. They also saw the plan as a colonialist, imperialist effort by several strong countries to take advantage of a much weaker people. They urged a united Arab effort to exterminate the Jews in Palestine. As the British began to withdraw, Arabs from the surrounding nations began to infiltrate Palestine. A guerrilla war between Jews and Arabs broke out, with a larger war seeming imminent as the days of the mandate dwindled down.

David Ben-Gurion and Golda Meir congratulate each other on the passage of the UN partition plan in 1947, which divided Palestine into a Jewish state and an Arab state. Both Jews and Arabs had reservations about the plan, however, and within a year a guerrilla war broke out between them.

In April 1948, with the two sides jockeying for control of key roads and villages in preparation for an all-out struggle, a battle occurred between a Haganah brigade and a Druze force over control of Kibbutz Ramat Yohanan and a nearby village. Though the Jews emerged victorious, among their losses was Dayan's younger brother, Zorik. A few days later, with the family still in mourning — Zorik, 22, had left behind a wife and infant child — word reached Moshe that the defeated Druze would consider ending their cooperation with the other hostile Arab forces. At the talks held to settle terms for their neutralization, the Druze were shocked to learn that Dayan was one of the primary negotiators in attendance — shocked because, according to Druze tradition, such a family loss could only be atoned for by revenge. In fact, the Druze even feared they had fallen into some sort of trap. But as those present recalled, Dayan told the ashen-faced Druze: "Since you have come to make a pact with us, I forgive you for spilling blood of my blood."

On May 14, 1948, the British high commissioner for Palestine departed, formally ending Britain's involvement in the country. That night, Ben-Gurion, speaking for the executive committee of the Jewish Agency and the Jewish National Council, proclaimed the establishment of the state of Israel. The next day the Arab armies of Egypt, Syria, Iraq, Transjordan, and Lebanon, along with contingents from Saudi Arabia, Sudan, and Yemen, declared war on the new nation.

One of the first targets of the Arab invasion was Degania, which in addition to its status as a preeminent kibbutz was also strategically situated at the northern entrance to the Jordan Valley. Dayan was put in charge of the kibbutz defense. The Israelis were not as well equipped as their adversaries. However, the Israeli soldiers, having benefited from their military association with Britain during World War II, were extremely well trained and disciplined — the small arms proved to be enough.

A Jerusalem resident reads a *Palestine Post* headline on May 14, 1948. The Israelis soon discovered that Israel's nationhood could not simply be announced but had to be fought for militarily and settled only after a long, complicated negotiation process.

The Arab losses were devastating. Estimates vary, but most sources suggest that nearly 700,000 Arabs were displaced by the conflict. Those whose villages were not razed fled to avoid the violence and hardship of war or left out of a refusal to live in a Jewish state. In his memoirs, former Israeli prime minister Yitzhak Rabin estimated that his unit alone forced 50,000 Arab civilians from their homes, driving most of them across the borders (Israel had expanded its borders by conquest beyond those established by the UN partition plan to include western Galilee, Jaffa, the new city of Jerusalem, and the corridor between Jerusalem and the coast). Thus, as with the Israelis, a yearning to return to the homeland from which they were forcibly evicted remains the unifying purpose of the Palestinian nationalist movement and is crucial to understanding the Israeli-Arab tensions as they exist today.

Dayan's military rehabilitation had begun on a triumphant note. He was then called upon to organize a commando unit — the 89th Battalion, which made major contributions to the war effort and helped the young state to solidify its new borders.

It was at this point that Dayan began to display the audacity and élan that would during the course of his career arouse so much criticism and at the same time prove so effective. Among the early stunts condoned by Dayan was the theft by his men of civilian jeeps — which were quickly painted army-issue khaki — as a way of equipping the platoon. The argument used to justify such questionable behavior was that supplies were short in prestate Israel.

The unit's first mission was to help the government deal with what has become known as the *Altalena* affair. The *Altalena* was a ship that had been chartered by Begin and the Irgun (with U.S. support) to sail from France to Israel carrying $5 million worth of much-needed arms and hundreds of willing fighters. Ben-Gurion recognized the need for such matériel but also saw the shipment as an Irgun challenge to the new government's authority. Dayan agreed, later saying, "This could only be viewed as an irresponsible and wanton defiance of government authority and had to be vigorously and speedily dealt with." The Irgun had always been the archrivals of the Haganah and had yet to lay down their arms and be absorbed into the Israeli army. Ben-Gurion even suspected that Begin — who had also opposed partition — might be planning some sort of grab for power.

Surviving *Altalena* crew members abandon ship. When the Irgun attempted to use the *Altalena* to bring arms and ammunition into Israel in violation of Israeli law, the Haganah shelled the vessel, exploding its $5 million cargo and killing more than 80 people.

As the boat tried to make its landing, Dayan's battalion was in place, along with others, to try and bring a peaceful resolution to the stand-off. However, it was not to be, as the rival groups exchanged fire — and charges of "who fired first." The ship burst into flames and more than 80 lives were lost.

Dayan did not remain on the scene for the duration of the conflict. At some point he was sent to the United States by Ben-Gurion to represent Israel at the West Point burial of David Marcus, an American Jew who had joined Israel's army and was killed in action. Some point out that Dayan's having been "excused" from seeing the *Altalena* affair to its finish was not simply the result of an innocent conflict of responsibilities but was instead a carefully considered maneuver to avoid having his reputation tarnished by a controversial episode; others defend Dayan, saying that he was not one to avoid controversy.

While in the United States, Dayan met Abraham Baum, a much-decorated American veteran of World War II. Baum enthralled Dayan with his tales of bravado and with his advice and strategies for aggressive mechanized warfare.

Upon his return to Israel, with the war still active on several fronts, Dayan put what he had learned into action. Operation Danny was at hand — part of which was a major offensive designed to push the Arab Legion of Transjordan away from the vicinity of Tel Aviv (Israel's major population center) and the Egyptian army away from Jewish settlements in the Negev Desert.

Just before the 89th Battalion moved out to capture the Arab village of Karatiya, Dayan ordered, "Nobody is to stop for anything or anybody. No assistance is to be given by anyone until we reach the wadi [dry river bed]. Nobody is to stop except by command or in order to open fire. Until we get to the wadi the order is advance, penetrate, move, move, move, all the time." The unit had already used full-frontal assaults to capture Dir Tarif, Lydda, and Ramle, helped along by the firepower of the Terrible Tiger, as the unit dubbed an armored car abandoned by the Transjordanians but captured — under sniper fire—and quickly repaired by the Israelis.

This emphasis on the offensive was a controversial way of waging war, especially for the Jews. What made it controversial was Dayan's apparent willingness to suffer large casualties despite the fact that there simply were not that many Jews, much less Jewish fighters, in the first place.

Dayan had brought another innovation to the Israel Defense Forces — that of the commander leading his forces into battle instead of directing the fight from behind. This credo — Follow me! — imbued men of all ranks with impressive self-confidence — often an army's best weapon. Indeed, commentators have often said that this high motivation, displayed by top commanders on down through the ranks, is among the factors that have made the Israel Defense Forces one of the premier armies in the world.

In any case, the 89th Battalion had another problem to deal with during the Karatiya operation. When the force reached the wadi the men realized that there had been a miscalculation — the gully's walls were too steep for any advance to be made. Dayan, at first worried by the halt in the operation, ordered several men to dig ramps to aid the passage, and then, as Egyptian artillery continued to light up the night, he surprised everyone by taking a nap. His reasoning was very sound — the digging would take a while, the men were fully capable of digging without his supervision, and he had not slept for days.

The assault was a success. By capturing Lydda and Ramle, Dayan had neutralized the threat posed by the pocket of Arab villages positioned uncomfortably close to Tel Aviv, the Tel Aviv–Jerusalem highway, and the airport at Lod. And the victory at Karatiya had dealt the Egyptians a setback and relieved pressure on Israel's Negev settlements. For his efforts Dayan was awarded the Jerusalem command.

Morale in Jerusalem was low. The city itself — which contained several sites sacred to Jews, including the Temple Mount, the Jewish Quarter, and the Western (or Wailing) Wall (the remains of Solomon's ancient temple) — was divided by an ugly, dangerous no-man's-land of mines, trenches, and barbed wire. Days and nights were punctuated by

Ben Yehuda Street, Jerusalem, in 1948, the year Dayan took over the Israeli army's Jerusalem command. Ironically, Jerusalem's status as a holy city for three major religions — Judaism, Christianity, and Islam — has often turned it into a battleground.

constant street battles, artillery barrages, and sniper fire. The Jewish Quarter of the Old City had already fallen to Transjordan, as had several other sectors of the city, and it was by no means certain that what remained in Jewish hands would stay that way. Mount Scopus, a hilltop enclave, was cut off from the rest of the city.

Armistice talks under the auspices of the United Nations were under way, both in Jerusalem and on the Greek island of Rhodes. Dayan became directly involved in these discussions, bringing to them a canny political sense he had not yet displayed. In fact, he and his Transjordanian counterpart in Jerusalem, Abdullah el-Tel, became very well acquainted, so much so that they were able to break through much of the diplomatic protocol that usually hinders the progress of such talks. At one point during seemingly stalled discussions, Dayan and el-Tel went off to talk on their own — the first time that Israeli and Arab leaders had met without the presence of a third party. Remarkably, they achieved an understanding concerning several issues and, more important, agreed to set up a direct telephone link for future communications between them. Among the things they discussed were the exact cease-fire lines, safe passage for workers to and from Mount Scopus, prisoner exchanges, access to holy places, and the delineation of a no-man's-land.

Dayan's forays with el-Tel were extremely successful in maintaining order in Jerusalem, a close-quartered, pressure cooker of a city. The two also established something of a personal rapport. Ruth Dayan wrote that el-Tel said of Moshe, "It is a good thing to have an enemy like your husband. We know that a word is a word." And Dayan later wrote, "El-Tel impressed me as being far superior to the other Arab officers and political functionaries."

As amenable as the talks may have been, however, these were discussions between representatives of two countries legally at war. Further, el-Tel did not have complete support for his contacts with the Jews. Thus, at one point he asked Dayan if he could arrange for the *Palestine Post*, a Jewish newspaper, to run attacks on him as a way of bolstering his anti-Israeli credentials.

El-Tel did have support in the right places, though. In 1949, King Abdullah himself invited Dayan to his palace at Shuneh, near the Dead Sea, for the first of several peace talks. Over the next two years, Dayan and other high-ranking Israeli officials met frequently with Abdullah, journeying secretly by night to Shuneh and to Amman, the Jordanian capital, a longer and more dangerous trip. Dayan would remove his eye patch and wear dark sunglasses so as not to be recognized. On one occasion, Dayan and another Israeli had to hide in the back seat, covered by an Arab headdress, so as to escape detection.

Discussions of cease-fire terms and other issues affecting the tense borders between the two countries began. The talks were sometimes productive, sometimes not. Ultimately, however, Abdullah paid for his willingness to contemplate full peace (as opposed to the armistice being negotiated at Rhodes) with the Jewish state. On July 22, 1951, upon emerging from Jerusalem's el-Aksa Mosque, he was assassinated. "He was a king," Dayan wrote, "but he was unable to achieve what he wished to achieve." The line serves as a fitting epitaph.

On July 20, the last of the armistice agreements with Israel's neighbors was signed. Israel was a state — surrounded by hostile nations, to be sure, but a state nonetheless.

4

Soldier, Minister, Private Citizen

In October 1949, Dayan was promoted to brigadier general and put in charge of the southern command, in the Negev Desert, an area encompassing nearly half of Israel and the site of much of the Jews' prehistory. Desolate and harsh, the region was something of a mystery to most Israelis but was becoming home to more and more immigrants. It was also a danger zone, with vast spaces and hidden canyons that gave wide freedom of movement to the many Arab militants who, in defiance of the armistice agreements, stole across the borders from Jordan and Egypt.

Not surprisingly, Dayan felt a pressing need to familiarize himself with the land, and so he rode deep into the wilderness, exploring and documenting its physical contours. Noting the stark beauty of the Negev, he wrote, "It was a wide-open expanse, bare, parched, craggy, primeval, yielding only the tropical acacia and tamarisk and a bush with long hard thorns, sharp as spears. It was quite unlike the northern Israel I knew, which seemed to me now to be a soft garden in delicate flower. There was also a strength about the features of the Negev unmatched by those in the north."

Dayan demonstrates his knowledge of firearms for his daughter, Yael, who is wearing an Israeli army uniform, and his son Assaf in 1959. In Israel, military service is mandatory for women as well as for men.

Such trips only increased Dayan's love for his native land. At the same time, the Negev and its development provided Dayan with a real-life training ground — as a soldier and as a statesman. "My activities were . . . quite varied. I would review tank maneuvers, call on new immigrants from Yemen who had just settled in, visit a border kibbutz which had become the target of infiltrators, follow the construction of a road through the Arava, inspect the training of reservists, check on the development of Eilat, and give constant thought both to hastening civilian growth and to strengthening our defenses by the more effective utilization of the small forces at our disposal."

One of the most important lessons the Negev taught Dayan was that an Israeli military presence on the frontier was crucial for Israel's security and peace with Egypt. This lesson was underscored in 1952 when Gamal Abdel Nasser, a staunch Arab nationalist, ousted Egypt's King Farouk in a coup and came to office calling for, among other things, a policy of confrontation with Israel.

At the end of 1951, Dayan attended a three-month military course at the Senior Officers' School at Devizes in England. Upon his return he was given a new command post, in the north, responsible for Galilee and the Hula Valley. By his progress it was apparent that Dayan had been taken under the wing of David Ben-Gurion.

Ben-Gurion was a Russian-Polish Jew who had once boasted as a child, "One day I will be the leader of Israel." After arriving in Palestine in 1906 he quickly set out to make this dream a reality. First working as a farm laborer (in the best tradition of the early Zionist settlers), he later helped to found Hashomer, the first Jewish defense organization in modern times. During World War I he was expelled from Palestine by the Turks and ended up fighting with the English against them. Upon his return to the Holy Land following the war he became one of the founders of the Haganah and also of the Histradut, the General Federation of Jewish Labor. Such activism led to his position as the leader of the Yishuv and to the primacy of his brand of Labor

Zionism. During the 1930s and 1940s he clashed often with the British over their policies in Palestine and also with Chaim Weizmann over Weizmann's "Anglocentric" diplomatic strategy (though they were allies in their Zionist ideology). In 1948, Ben-Gurion became Israel's first prime minister.

Dayan had already proven himself to Ben-Gurion with his exploits during the War of Independence and earlier. Commentators say, too, that Dayan displayed some of the same qualities people admired in Ben-Gurion — fortitude, a flair for daring-yet-prudent actions, and an ability to inspire others to their full potential. Whatever the case, the two were to prosper through cooperation with each other over the years, even if at times Dayan would challenge his superior.

Their relationship had one of its many climaxes on December 6, 1953, when Ben-Gurion appointed Dayan chief of staff, the second-highest post in the Israeli armed forces. The very next day, Ben-Gurion resigned. He had planned to do so for a couple of years, to prove, as he put it, that "no one is indispensable to a state." He departed for Sde Boker, a kibbutz in a remote part of the Negev, hoping to inspire others to do likewise and leave the cities to become pioneers.

Dayan was pleased with his new job, but not everyone rejoiced. There were many critics of the appointment who felt he was too unruly and too inexperienced for the job. Some even went so far as

David Ben-Gurion (center, with bent arm), at the Rishon le-Sion settlement in Palestine, where in 1907 he worked as a farm laborer. Ben-Gurion, a Russian-Polish Jew, vowed at a very young age that someday he would be the leader of a Jewish state.

Ben-Gurion ceremoniously appoints Dayan chief of staff, the second highest Israeli military post, in 1953. Also pictured (left to right) are Major General Mordechai Makleff, Dayan's predecessor; Lieutenant Colonel Nehemia Arg'ov; and Moshe Sharett, who replaced Ben-Gurion as prime minister that year.

to say that Ben-Gurion had been irresponsible in selecting Dayan. However, Dayan was to prove his detractors wrong.

Dayan put into effect some immediate changes: He turned his office into a kind of conference room, more closely resembling a field station than an office, and he kept the door to it open at all times so as to be more accessible to the men. Out in the field Dayan wore fatigues and sat on the ground with the troops, getting "dirty and sultry" with them, as he put it. He also made it a habit to conduct inspections personally, often at night and without advance notice, believing that to do so was the best way to see for himself whether or not Israeli troops were as they should be — in a constant state of readiness. Finally, he initiated a more aggressive policy of conducting retaliatory operations. In other words, he "took the fight to the enemy" instead of remaining on the defensive. Israel's neighbors had left Dayan no choice. The armistice agreements signed several years earlier had brought not peace but an upsurge in border infiltrations.

In May 1951, Dayan was told of an Israeli retaliatory raid that had retreated, without accomplishing its objective, after suffering some casualties. Dayan was shocked at what he felt was the low level of intensity shown by the unit. As chief of staff he was determined that such a failure not be allowed to recur, and so he instituted a new rule: No mission was to be aborted until casualties (killed and wounded combined) amounted to at least 50 percent. This apparent willingness on Dayan's part to tolerate the loss of Jewish lives was very controversial and reminded people of Dayan's philosophy of full-frontal attacks during the War of Independence. As then, military necessity carried the day. Israel's armed forces had to be that much more spirited than their enemies. However, many people also began to question the concept of retaliation, seeing the violence as part of a never-ending, escalating circle of attack and reprisal.

In 1953, Dayan organized Force 101, a volunteer commando unit with Ariel Sharon at its head. According to Teveth the men of Force 101 "dressed as they pleased, in short pants, white or colored shirts, multicolored *keffiyot* [peaked caps], berets, and beards; they were armed with tommy guns (rather than regulation Zahal [as the Israeli army was called in Hebrew] arms), Molotov cocktails [homemade hand grenades], and commando knives; and they wore no rank insignia. The total disregard for etiquette, spit and polish, inspection, and military hierarchy must certainly have endeared the men of 101 to Dayan."

What also appealed to Dayan was the unit's fighting spirit. Sometimes, though, zeal could be carried to an extreme. Such was the case, many felt, with an operation launched in response to a grenade attack on an Israeli home in which a mother and her two children were killed.

The Jordanian town of Qibya, located directly across the border from the Israeli town that had been attacked, was selected as the target. Following a plan devised by Dayan, Force 101 entered the town on the night of October 14, intending to destroy about 50 homes as punishment. Instead 69 people, mostly women and children who had taken cover in the homes that were to be blown up, lost their lives, prompting an international outcry.

To some Israelis, the raid showed that Dayan had put Israeli forces into good shape and had put fear into the enemy. To others the incident was a terrorist act and a shameful degeneration of Jewish principles. Dayan, though he was said to have felt that this incident was characteristic of wartime and that he was not sorry it had happened, would later

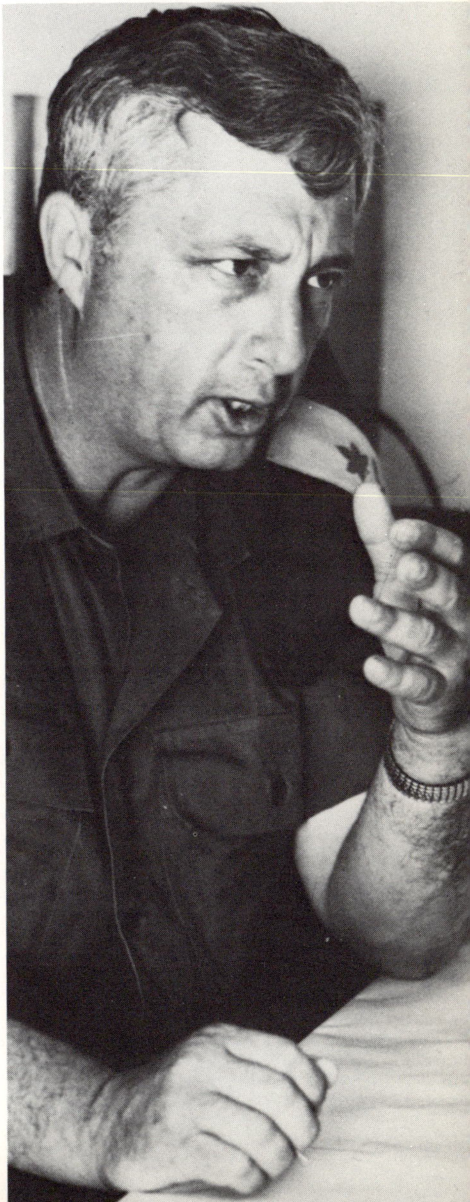

General Ariel Sharon, leader of Force 101, a commando unit founded by Dayan in 1953. On October 14 of that year, Force 101 raided the Jordanian town of Qibya, killing 69 people, mostly women and children. Public outcry over the incident forced Dayan to rethink the army's retaliation policy.

Egyptian president Gamal Abdel Nasser, in 1955, the year he closed the Strait of Tiran to Israeli shipping. The move blocked Israel's access to essential goods and military supplies and foreshadowed Nasser's 1956 attempt to nationalize the Suez Canal, thereby threatening the transport of oil to Israel and other nations.

change the policy of retaliation so that only military objectives and targets would be considered.

Tensions between Israel and its Arab neighbors reached another crescendo in 1955. In September, Nasser blockaded the Strait of Tiran, cutting off Israel's shipping outlet to Africa and Asia, through which essential goods and military supplies normally traveled. Also that month, Nasser concluded an agreement with Czechoslovakia to obtain a level and scale of Soviet-bloc arms unprecedented for Egypt, and this posed a direct challenge to Israel. Dayan called the deal "a stunning acceleration of the pace of rearmament in the Middle East."

Dayan and his political and military superiors began to draw up plans for an anticipatory strike or preemptive war. In March 1956 Dayan warned that war would break out before the end of the year. Four months later, President Nasser stunned the world by nationalizing the Suez Canal.

England and France were among the many nations who depended on the right of free passage through the canal for the goods — especially oil — that were needed to keep their industrialized societies running and also for their conduct of commercial trade. Nasser's move jeopardized that passage. France was already displeased with Nasser for his support for anti-French rebels in Algeria, where France ruled as a colonial power. Israel, needless to say, was the most concerned of all, not just by the threat to free shipping but by the heightened likelihood of war with the Egyptians. By late October, with Egypt having formed a joint military command with Syria and Jordan, an outbreak of fighting was all but inevitable.

France and England wanted to mount a military intervention, but held off at the behest of American secretary of state John Foster Dulles. Still, France's minister of defense could not resist approaching Shimon Peres, the director-general of Israel's Ministry of Defense, who had established excellent contacts with high-ranking French military officials through arms deals between the two countries. In Paris shortly after Nasser's seizure of the canal, Peres was asked, "How much time do you think it would take for your army to cross the Sinai Peninsula and reach the Suez?" From this simple question ensued something much more involved — the Sinai Campaign.

With Dayan, Ben-Gurion (who had been reelected prime minister in November 1955), and Peres making frequent trips to Paris, a plan was devised for Israeli troops to initiate an attack and seize the region; the British and French were to join the fighting later by landing paratroopers at Port Said, the northern entry to the canal, thereby seizing control of the entire waterway. According to a French military official who took part in the discussions, "Dayan's clear and dynamic attitude was most striking. He knew exactly what he wanted and what it was in his power to achieve."

As Dayan himself wrote, "Our objectives were to neutralize the armed Egyptian threat, end the *fedayeen* [suicide squad] terrorism from the Gaza Strip, and gain control of one pinpoint of land, Sharm el-Sheikh, near the southern tip of the peninsula. By capturing Sharm, we would automatically break the Egyptian blockade of the Gulf of Aqaba." Actually, Dayan didn't want the British or French to be involved; Israel, he felt, could do the job perfectly well on its own. Ben-Gurion, it was said, agreed to major power involvement so as to win Israel important allies.

On October 29, Dayan launched the Sinai Campaign with a paratroop drop at the eastern entrance

to the Mitla Pass, one of two strategic byways in the western Sinai. At the same time, an armed brigade embarked down the coast toward Sharm el-Sheikh. To the Egyptians, the actions looked like the beginning of a retaliatory raid — which is exactly what Dayan had hoped. As a further diversionary tactic Dayan had also concentrated a good amount of Israeli troops on the Israel-Jordan border. In this way Israel achieved total surprise.

Dayan's strategic and tactical brilliance was evident throughout the Sinai Campaign. Dayan ordered the forward drop in Mitla so that Israel could capture its final objective at the war's very outset; this unorthodox method thoroughly disrupted the Egyptian army, which was much more comfortable fighting a force attacking head-on. Likewise, the Israelis' dash down the Gulf of Aqaba coastline was intended to further bewilder the Egyptians with sheer speed; this, too, unsettled the Egyptians and nullified their huge advantages in personnel and matériel.

Israel easily routed the Egyptians. However, the Anglo-French part of the plan did not go as planned; in fact, their assault on Port Said was too little too late. Dayan said of the French effort that it was "a complete flop." By this time, too, the campaign had become an international crisis, with the United States arguing for a cease-fire. After 10 days of action, with Israel in complete control of the Sinai and the British and French holding Port Said, the fighting came to a halt.

Dayan seemed to have been at every critical battle during the campaign. At one point, too impatient with sitting in Tel Aviv waiting for news of the attack on Sharm el-Sheikh, Dayan decided to go there himself. He arrived somewhat prematurely — to the sight of hundreds of armed Egyptian soldiers walking in his direction. These were retreating troops who had just lost the battle for Sharm el-Sheikh; luckily for Dayan and his few companions, the Egyptians moved on without noticing him and without firing, even though Dayan was standing in the back of the Jeep in full view. "They simply let us pass by, their faces a study in feebleness and exhaustion," Dayan wrote.

Dayan was back at Sharm el-Sheikh on March 7, 1957, to accompany his troops in evacuating the area as part of Israel's agreed-upon withdrawal from the Sinai. Under intense pressure from U.S. president Dwight D. Eisenhower, and in the face of six UN resolutions, Israel had decided to withdraw from the region. UN forces were to be placed between the Israelis and Egyptians to put an end to the fedayeen raids, and the United States promised to help keep the Gulf of Aqaba and the Strait of Tiran open. Israelis swallowed this bitter pill, and many of them said that the next time they occupied territory as a result of a defensive war, they would withdraw only in exchange for a treaty of peace. Nonetheless, the Sinai Campaign made Dayan a national hero.

Ben-Gurion was again the nation's choice for prime minister in 1959, and he selected Dayan as the new minister of agriculture. Since the victory in the Sinai, Dayan had resigned from the army and begun to study political science at the Hebrew University in Jerusalem. Not surprisingly, Dayan became a controversial rising star in Israeli politics.

According to Harry Sachar, author of *A History of Israel*, Dayan as minister of agriculture "coined a phrase destined to have far-reaching impact in public discussions. He asked for a shift in emphasis from pioneering to state efficiency. Technocracy and meritocracy, he argued, not seniority and ideology, should henceforth be the guiding principles of modern administration." This was perceived as an attack by the so-called young guard on those who

Israeli forces on the Sinai Peninsula. In response to Nasser's nationalization of the Suez Canal, Israel launched an attack on Egypt. After only eight days of fighting, Israel was able to occupy both the Gaza Strip and the Sinai Peninsula, but Ben-Gurion withdrew the troops under pressure from the United Nations.

had founded the state. This did not endear Dayan to many of his superiors, at times Ben-Gurion included. Dayan did, meanwhile, turn in an effective stint in office. Farmers' income rose by 6 percent during his first year in office and 20 percent during his second, reversing the declining trend that had preceded him.

In June 1963, Ben-Gurion resigned once and for all. Complex political jockeying accompanied his decision. Levi Eshkol, one of the settlers at Degania and a long-term figure in *Mapai*, Israel's workers' party, was Ben-Gurion's handpicked successor as both prime minister and minister of defense. Dayan had his doubts about being able to serve Eshkol, as Eshkol was allied with others whose social and economic policies he opposed. Three months later Dayan submitted his resignation to the prime minister, some say as an effort to gain strength through a battle of wills. Dayan was convinced to stay on, but by November 1964, increasingly critical of Eshkol's handling of the country's economy, he resigned again, this time for good.

Ben-Gurion broke with Eshkol in February 1965 because of the latter's unwillingness to conduct an investigation into an embarrassing national security mishap that had occurred years earlier. He formed a breakaway party known as Rafi and enticed Shimon Peres and many of the young guard to join. Dayan was reluctant at first, to the point of being accused of betrayal on the front page of *Yediot Aharonot*, an Israeli newspaper, and being chided by many for thinking of himself first. After all, the political fortunes of the new party were decidedly questionable. Dayan weighed the decision carefully

Ben-Gurion pins the Haganah medal on Moshe Dayan in June 1958. The success of the Sinai campaign made Dayan a national hero.

and several months later joined the party. In that year's elections, however, the party won only 10 seats, and Dayan soon withdrew from the front lines of his country's politics.

The following year, Dayan decided to visit Vietnam, where American forces were engaged in an (ultimately futile) effort to help South Vietnam prevent North Vietnamese communists from taking over the country. "I wanted to see for myself, on the spot, what modern war was like," he wrote, "how the new weaponry was handled, how it shaped up in action, whether it could be adapted for our own use."

Dayan prepared for his journey by meeting with prominent military officials in several countries: French general de Castries, who had commanded French forces during their defeat at Dien Bien Phu in 1954; Britain's field marshal Bernard Montgomery; U.S. secretary of defense Robert McNamara; and General Maxwell Taylor, then chairman of the U.S. joint chiefs of staff.

Accredited as a journalist, Dayan wrote some newspaper articles for the *Washington Post* and *Maariv* and accompanied American troops into action. The Egyptians accused him of preparing for war; actually, as Dayan soon found upon his return from Asia, it was the Egyptians themselves who were.

Dayan accompanies a U.S. Marine reconnaissance patrol in Vietnam in 1966. Dayan went to Southeast Asia, where U.S. forces were fighting the North Vietnamese, to observe U.S. strategies and weaponry in action.

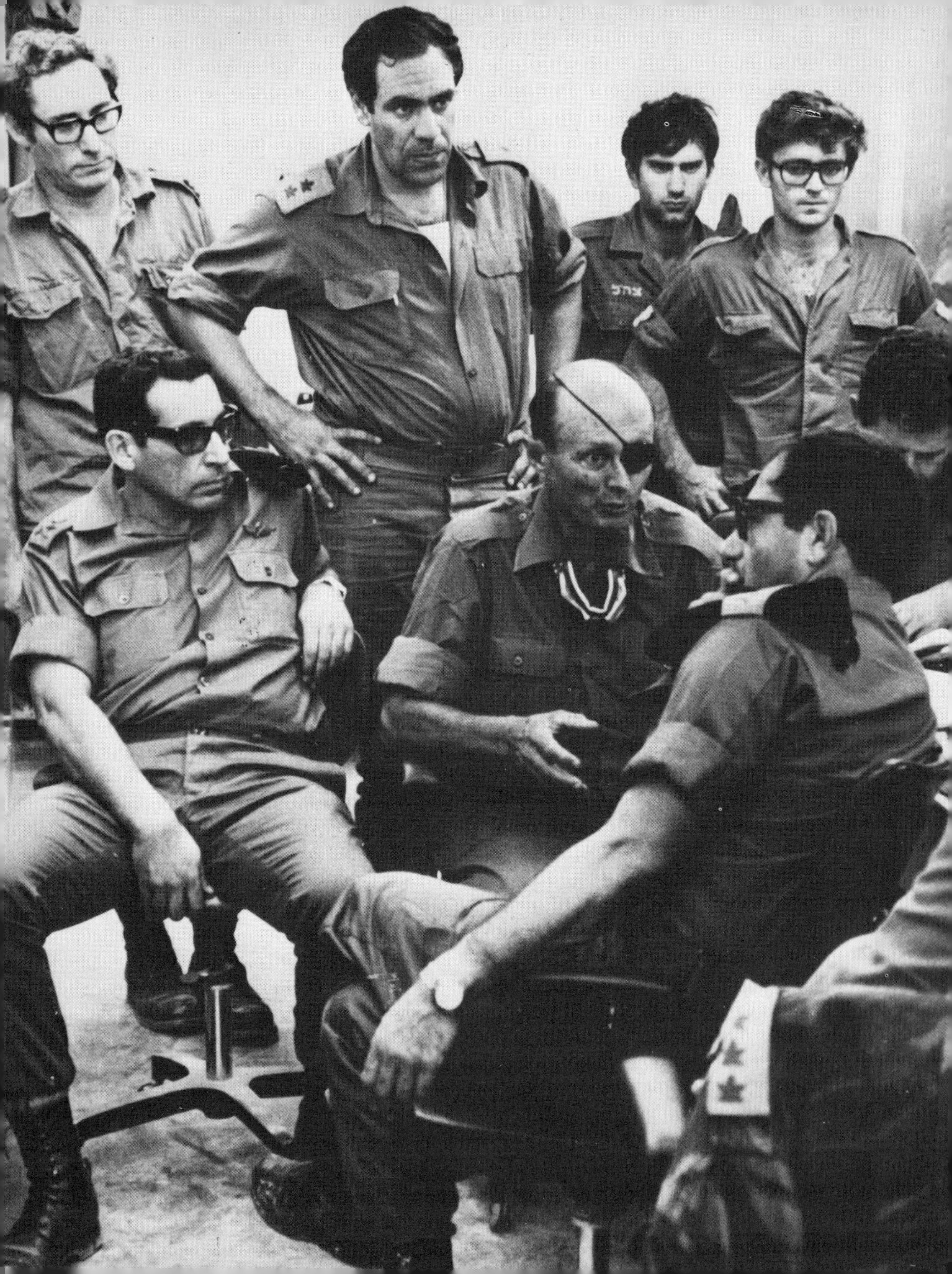

5

Six Days That Changed the World

We intend to open a general assault against Israel. This will be total war. Our basic aim is the destruction of Israel." So spoke Egypt's president Gamal Abdel Nasser in late May 1967, as Egypt, along with Syria, Jordan, and several other Arab states, prepared for a joint military effort against the Jewish state.

Nasser, always a leading spokesman on behalf of Arab nationalism and against Israel, had "raised the ante" by taking several steps that seemed to place his country and Israel on a violent collision course: First, he forced the removal of United Nations peacekeeping forces from the Sinai Peninsula, the "buffer zone" between Egypt and Israel where the UN troops had been stationed since the 1956 hostilities between the two countries; second, he moved more than 80,000 Egyptian troops and convoys of armaments into the area; third, he blockaded the Gulf of Aqaba and the Strait of Tiran, Israel's vital shipping route to Asia and elsewhere; and finally, he concluded military alliances with Jordan, Syria, and Iraq, all avowed enemies of Israel.

> *Our only objective is to thwart the attempts of the Arab armies to conquer our country.*
> —MOSHE DAYAN

Dayan meets with Israeli general Shmuel Gonen and other military personnel during the Six-Day War. Dayan spearheaded Israel's capture of the Sinai Peninsula, the Golan Heights, the West Bank of the Jordan River, and East Jerusalem, making Israel the Middle East's dominant military power.

Virtually the entire Arab world joined Nasser in issuing rhetoric calling for vengeance and jihad (Arabic for holy war). Arab intentions could not have been any clearer. As Dayan later commented, "Even those who tended to discount the florid phraseology of Arab leaders could not seal their ears against the whooping war cries that burst forth." To the people of Israel, such words and actions meant only one thing—war.

The question facing the country was not whether Egypt would attack but what could be done in the face of this certainty. Should Israel wait for Egypt to strike, absorb the first blow, and then hit back with force? Did Israel have the strength to take such a chance? Or should Israel mount a preemptive attack, thereby blunting the enemy's overwhelming superiority in personnel and weaponry? This tactic had a different risk — that of being labeled the country that shot first. And what were the prospects for diplomacy? Could Israel count on its major allies to help bring about a peaceful resolution to the crisis?

As Israelis considered these questions, a sense of impending doom pervaded the country. Newspapers in and out of Israel wrote that the state seemed "on the brink of extinction." The public was clamoring for a government of "national unity" to deal with Israel's gravest crisis yet. Adding to the sense of emergency was the relative surprise Nasser's declarations had provoked in Dayan and in the Armed Forces Intelligence Service. Both had thought Egyptian forces too occupied with the civil war in Yemen to be able to contemplate war with Israel. (Egypt had sent troops to support "republican" revolutionaries there against the "royalists" backed by Saudi Arabia. This had caused military friction between Egypt and Saudi Arabia and cast a pall over Nasser's ideal of Arab unity.) Dayan, in April, had said that war with Israel's southern neighbor was some 10 years off.

Aggravating the threat from abroad was a leadership vacuum within. Lieutenant General Yitzhak Rabin, commander in chief of the armed forces, was ill. He had suffered either a temporary nervous breakdown or simple exhaustion brought on, some said, by his despair at the situation. Worse, Prime Minister Levi Eshkol was indecisive. During the crisis, Eshkol delivered a radio address that was intended to calm Israeli fears, to assure them that the government and military were in control of the situation. The speech was a disaster. Reading the badly typed pages of a hurriedly prepared speech, Eshkol stuttered, fumbled, and stammered his way through — apparent incompetence when the public had been hoping for deliverance.

A newspaper editorial the following day summarized the mood of the country following the speech: "[Eshkol] is not constituted to be prime minister and minister of defense in the present situation. The proposal that Ben-Gurion be entrusted with the premiership and Moshe Dayan with the ministry of defense, while Eshkol is given charge of domestic affairs, seems . . . wise."

Dayan had been out of the army for 10 years and out of the political fray for 3. Yet the public remembered his earlier achievements, in particular the 1956 campaign but more generally the feeling of self-confidence he was so able to transmit to the men under his charge. They wanted him appointed minister of defense without a moment's delay. Even Menachem Begin, the Labor party's longtime archrival, agreed.

Dayan and Lieutenant General Yitzhak Rabin, commander in chief of the Israeli armed forces, in 1967.

An incredible degree of political maneuvering ensued. One exchange between Eshkol and Dayan, which took place on May 31, 1957, serves as an example. Eshkol asked Dayan if he was willing to become the deputy prime minister of a government of national unity and, if not, whether there was some other post he would accept. Dayan replied, "That's a hypothetical question; therefore, the answer will be too. I am prepared to be prime minister or minister of defense or both. If I cannot be in charge of defense affairs, then I would like to be mobilized, but this would be outside any political negotiations. In that case I would be prepared to assume any post the chief of staff decides upon." Eshkol then asked which specific post he had in mind. Dayan replied, "Chief of southern command, because I know Sinai and the Egyptians well. But in the army, I would even be willing to drive a half-track."

At first, Eshkol was not willing to give up his posts. There were also some people calling for the return of Ben-Gurion as prime minister, defense minister, or both. Dayan himself remained away from the fray. The machinations were very complicated and involved and all the more remarkable considering the fact that war was imminent.

On June 2, Moshe Dayan was made minister of defense. The *New York Times* later wrote that "news of his appointment immediately restored the confidence of the armed forces and of the nation at large." Dayan was more modest: "This was the first time I would be acting without being subject to higher authority. . . . For good or ill, this was how the wheel had turned. In this war I would be on my own."

Even before being called in as minister of defense, Dayan had taken it upon himself to review his country's state of readiness. For two weeks in May he traveled throughout the Sinai, visiting the military outposts which would most likely face the Egyptian onslaught and the towns and kibbutzim that would also feel the fighting most directly. As he later wrote in his autobiography, "I wanted to get my teeth into what was happening in the line."

Dayan found that the operational plans being re-lied on for the coming assault were inadequate. He knew the Sinai and knew for the most part (with the aid of Israeli intelligence) what the Egyptian army was planning to do. He drew up new fighting instructions and a less formulaic battle plan that stressed the initiative of individual Israeli com-manders. "[The operational plans] lacked what I considered an essential Israeli element—compelling the Egyptian army to change its plans and deploy-ment," he wrote. "One of our basic advantages over the enemy was our ability to improvise during the course of a battle and to do so quickly. Thus, our plans should have been designed to create situa-tions in which the Egyptians would have to make operational changes, which they would do slowly and ineffectually."

Dayan holds a press confer-ence on June 3, 1967, in Tel Aviv, after accepting the post of minister of defense. Two days later, Israel was at war with Egypt.

Eshkol and the cabinet accepted Dayan's thinking with little debate. Meanwhile, a diplomatic solution looked less and less likely. Approaches to France, Great Britain, Canada, and the United States that were aimed at deterring Egypt from its course had elicited only lukewarm support. The United States, for its part, had wanted to mount an international flotilla that would make its way through the Suez Canal as a way of asserting the international community's — and therefore Israel's — right to freedom of passage. Considered ineffectual by many, however, and beset with logistical difficulties, this never happened.

The Israeli government then called for a total military mobilization. This meant, among other things, that there would be no more bus service — all available vehicles were to be used for military transport — and that public parks were sanctified by rabbis so that they could be used as emergency cemeteries. On Sunday, June 4, the Israeli cabinet approved a preemptive strike to be mounted the following morning.

At dawn the next day, Dayan walked over to and entered the air force command post. Minutes later, the war began. Shortly after 7:00 on the morning of June 5, 1967, Israeli warplanes moved out over the Mediterranean Sea and entered Egyptian air space, flying so low that they avoided radar detection. With lightning speed and remarkable accuracy, they proceeded to destroy more than 300 of Egypt's warplanes — most of its entire air arsenal — all while on the ground. Superiority of the skies thus assured, Israeli forces drove on, exhorted by Dayan, who addressed his troops over the military radio station: "Soldiers of Israel. . . . We are a small nation, but strong; peace loving, yet ready to fight for our lives and our country. Our civilians in the rear will no doubt suffer. But the supreme effort will be demanded of you, the troops, fighting in the air, on land, and on sea. Soldiers of the Israel Defense Forces, on this day our hopes and our security rest with you."

Following the plans mapped out by Dayan, Israeli tanks and infantry fanned out across the Sinai and marched through the Gaza Strip, achieving the same success as the air force. And as the fighting spread to other fronts — Syria and Jordan, with help from several other Arab countries, had joined the invasion — the magnitude of Israel's victory began to take form.

As in 1956, Israel had virtually no difficulties chasing the Egyptians from the Sinai Peninsula and Gaza Strip. Interestingly, Dayan did not want to capture the Suez Canal, primarily because Nasser would never rest until he got it back. If instead the Israelis had moved forward to within a few miles of the canal and fortified their positions there, Nasser would perceive less of a threat — both to his country and to his prestige. However, so quick was the Israelis' advance when war broke out that Dayan was presented with the canal without resistance.

From Syria, Israel captured the Golan Heights, which Syria had used for years to shell Israeli settlements in the valley below. Here, too, Dayan had been significantly more cautious than his war-hawk image would have one believe. He felt that storming

73

and taking the Golan would cost too many Israeli lives. The Golan was, more or less, a wall facing the Sea of Galilee. Thus, the imposing fortification afforded by the natural lay of the land meant that even a furious, full-frontal assault held no guarantee of success. Then, too, many of Israel's troops, planes, and artillery were focused on Egypt. Dayan's thinking changed only when Egypt agreed to a cease-fire; suddenly, the manpower became available for the successful assault on the Golan. From Jordon, Israel captured Judea and Samaria — the West Bank of the Jordan River — and the eastern half of Jerusalem, including the Old City and its holy sites.

For most Israelis the highlight of the Six-Day War, as it came to be known, was the capture and reunification of Jerusalem. Since the founding of the state, the Old City had been off-limits to the Jews. As the Arab Legion of Jordan was routed, Israeli soldiers rushed to the area of the Western Wall, made sure the area was safe, and then broke out in song and prayer, meanwhile jostling to touch the sacred stones. They were soon joined by Dayan, who, ironically, had not wanted to capture the Old City, again for fear of heavy casualties.

Exhausted Israeli soldiers rest in a grove of trees in Metulla, Israel, with the end of the 1967 Six-Day War in sight. One result of Israel's victory over the Arab forces was that for the first time in 2,000 years all of Jerusalem belonged to the Jews.

Still, the idea that Jerusalem, and, by extension, so much of the Jews' ancient heritage, would be back in Jewish hands was very, very powerful. As Dayan wrote, recalling the moment in his memoirs, "Throughout all the generations, during the two thousand years of their exile, the Jewish people had yearned for Jerusalem. It was the object of their pilgrimage, their dreams, their longings." In addition, the facts on the ground forced the issue. Israeli forces controlled all the high points around the Old City, making its capture inevitable. And so Dayan joined in the jubilation. He also followed Jewish tradition by placing a piece of paper in between the cracks of the wall — as did ancient pilgrims beseeching God to answer their prayers — on which was written a simple message: "May peace be upon all of Israel."

In just six days an outnumbered Israel had overwhelmed the Arabs, winning one of the greatest military victories in history, and Moshe Dayan, having reached another crest in an already spectacular career, had become the most popular man in a land that had known no shortage of heroes.

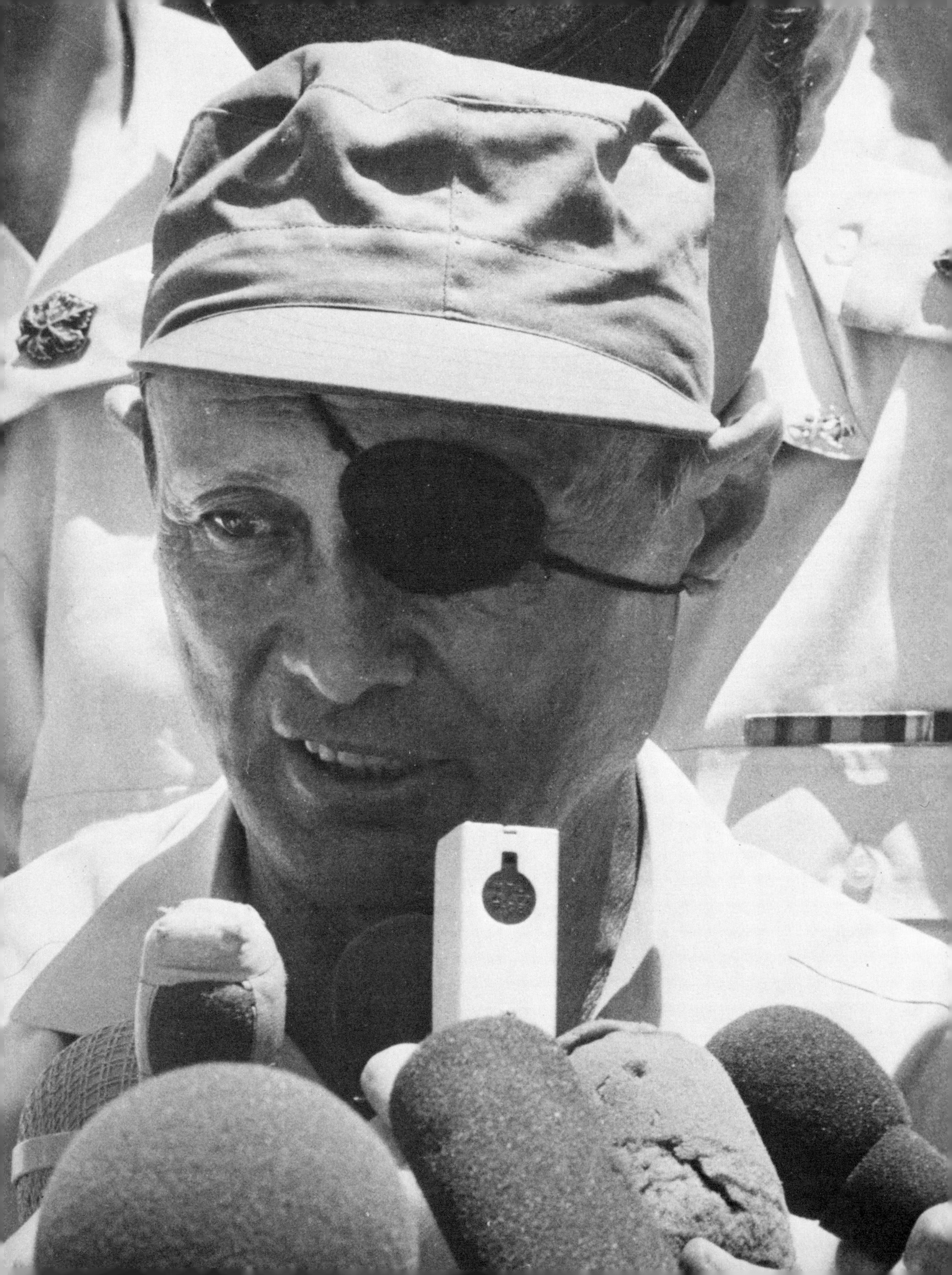

6

Setback

Following Israel's spectacular success in the Six-Day War, Dayan addressed the *mukhtars*, or village leaders, of the West Bank, Gaza Strip, and Golan Heights: "We do not ask you to love us. We ask only that you care for your own people and work with us in restoring the normalcy of their lives." He knew that troubled times lay ahead. One writer likened the task Israel now faced — of ruling over the one and a half million Arabs in the occupied territories — to "trying to hold on to and control the thrashing tail of an agitated whale."

In the wake of the victory, Dayan and others in power were of two minds. On the one hand, they said they were ready to trade the lands they had won in exchange for peace agreements. On the other hand, they said they would never return to pre-1967 borders. They waited for word to come — from King Hussein of Jordan, or any of their other Arab neighbors. Instead the Arab leaders responded in August by issuing the "three no's" — no peace, no recognition, no negotiations.

At a July 1973 press conference at Lod International Airport in Tel Aviv, Dayan tells reporters that he believes Arab guerrillas were responsible for the killing of Yosef Allon, the Israeli attaché in Washington. Dayan and others were awaiting the arrival of Allon's casket.

The Middle East. The former region of Palestine encompassed what is now Israel and the occupied territories (the West Bank, Golan Heights, and Gaza Strip).

Dayan, as minister of defense, became de facto military governor of the occupied territories. He began with dramatic overtures in Jerusalem: He stripped away the no-man's-land and opened the gates of the Old City so that there would be free movement between the city's eastern and western parts, and he allowed the Temple Mount, with its two mosques, to remain under the control of the Arabs. In Hebron he made arrangements for religious coexistence in the Cave of the Machpelah, where the patriarchs of biblical days, sacred to both Jews and Arabs, are said to be buried. He also instituted an open-bridges policy by which Arabs of Israel and the occupied territories could maintain contact with their Arab brethren.

Dayan's policy in the occupied territories is said by some to have been ahead of its time in that even today many Israelis are not as forthcoming toward the Arabs as he was then. The issue of what Israel should do about the territories it occupied in 1967 and the Palestinian population therein was then and remains today the crux of the entire Arab-Israeli conflict. There are those who favor the areas' annexation to the state of Israel. They reason that the land belongs only to the Jews, since it was the scene of so much of their biblical history. The Palestinians, meanwhile, argue for a state of their own on this land, with its capital in East Jerusalem. The land is theirs, too, they say, and has been for years. Another obstacle to peace is the Arabs' continued unwillingness to recognize the state of Israel and its right to exist. Some say that Israel, by wanting to hold onto these territories, has turned a great victory into a historical disaster. Others say that Israel can do no less in its search for security. With time the situation appears to many to have become more and more intractable. In any case, Dayan would remain among his country's liberals on the Arab question for most of his political career.

Anti-Israeli protesters demonstrate in front of the Israeli mission to the United Nations in New York City in February 1969. Some display a Palestine Liberation Organization (PLO) coat of arms while others carry signs equating Zionism with Nazism.

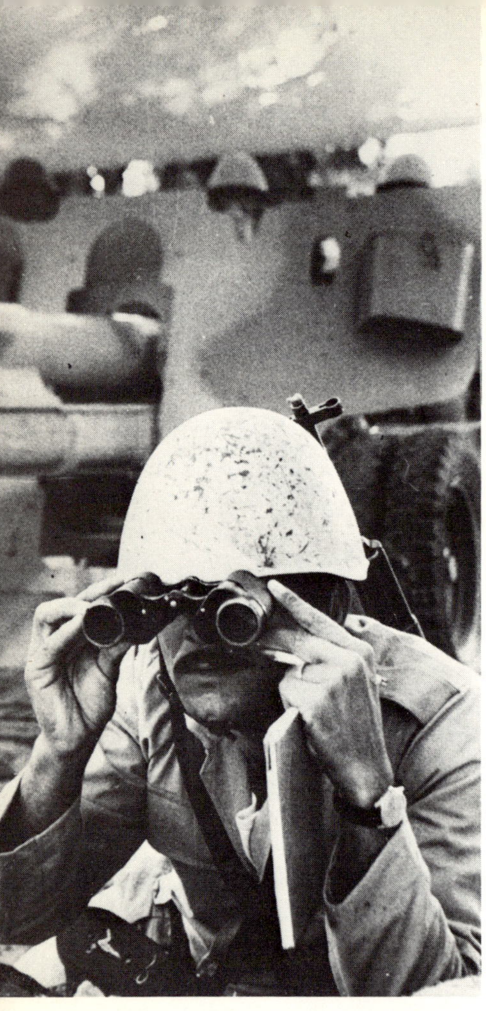

A United Arab Republic soldier on the west bank of the Suez Canal. Though the Arabs were beaten decisively by the Israelis in the battle over the canal, Nasser emerged a national hero for defying Israel and its powerful Western allies.

Meanwhile, Egypt's president Nasser remained committed to his aggressive stance toward Israel. Thus, he set out to regain by attrition what his armies had failed to do in outright war. (He was also trying to rehabilitate his reputation, which had been dealt a severe blow.) Nasser was able to mount this war of attrition, as it came to be called, because of the massive infusions of arms Egypt had received from the Soviet Union. The primary tactic involved artillery exchanges across the canal, aimed mostly at Israeli shipping and other military or commercial targets. Unlike Egypt, however, Israel lacked population centers in the canal zone; one instance of Israeli retaliation sparked the evacuation of tens of thousands of people from Suez City and Ismailia. Still, Nasser was at least partially right — the shelling would cost Dayan and Israel dearly. By the time a cease-fire was put in place in August 1970, 721 Israelis had been killed, as opposed to 790 in the entire Six-Day War.

Dayan also had to suppress terrorist infiltrations from Jordan. As it turned out, the Palestinians operating from Jordanian territory ended up posing a greater threat to the rule of King Hussein than to the Israelis. (The majority of Jordan's population is Palestinian.) By September 1970, Hussein had survived attempts on his life and had good reason to fear a complete Palestinian insurrection. He brutally suppressed the guerrillas, with at least 2,000 of them losing their lives at the hands of the Jordanian army and the rest being expelled from the country. This was an unqualified boon to the Israelis, at least in the short term.

Along with these upheavals came one in Dayan's personal life as well. In 1971 he and Ruth were divorced, at her request. They had been estranged for quite some time, a state of affairs that Ruth described in her autobiography: "I am convinced Moshe has left the realm of private life and become a kind of public property that belongs to the entire nation. . . . I think I truly knew him better than anyone else does, and I certainly would not include him among the saints. But I believe in him."

Ruth Dayan went on to relate an encounter she had with a reporter following the divorce: "'Is Moshe today the same man he was when you married him thirty-seven years ago?' I was asked. 'Certainly not' I answered. And this fact accounts, I think, for the long road people travel between marriage and divorce. Sometimes people just do not know each other when they marry, but I knew Moshe and he knew me, as we were then. . . . I loved Moshe for his dedication and his simplicity. He is not to blame that his historical role has elevated him to dizzying heights since then, and this fact has so changed him."

Moshe agreed with Ruth about the changes that occur in people over time. He wrote, "There was no special happening or crisis that left our marriage stranded on a sandbar. It was the absence of the necessary communion of souls and the increasing feeling that we were strangers that fashioned a barrier between us." In 1973, Moshe married his long-time companion, Rahel.

On October 6, 1973, Moshe Dayan was again called to face what he knew best — war. At 4:00 that morning he was awakened by the ringing of his red bedside telephone. He was told that before sundown that day Egypt and Syria were going to launch an attack aimed at annihilation of the Jewish state. The Arabs had picked the holiest day of the Jewish year, Yom Kippur, the Day of Atonement, when most Jews the world over are in synagogue, praying and fasting, to attack.

Ironically, Yom Kippur offered almost ideal circumstances for a full mobilization of Israeli reserves: Because no one drove, the roads were clear; because there were no radio broadcasts, the air-

Israeli soldiers police a large group of Arabs at an identification center in Israeli-occupied Jordan, July 1969. During its occupation of Jordan, Israel enforced a strict curfew and took other security measures in an effort to combat Arab guerrilla activity.

Israeli tanks on patrol during the 1973 Yom Kippur War. That October, Egypt and Syria attacked Israel on Yom Kippur, the holiest day of the Jewish year, catching their enemy off guard.

waves were clear for the efficient dissemination of information about the mobilization; and because families were for the most part together, preparing for the mobilization was that much easier. Had the Arabs selected any other holiday, confusion would likely have ensued.

Still, the attack was unlike anything Israel had ever experienced in any of its wars. The Arabs had a 10 to 1 advantage in troops, were equipped with sophisticated Soviet-bloc weapons, and had the element of surprise in their favor. For the first hours of the battle, Israel came perilously close to disaster. Reports of very heavy casualties soon began to reach the Israeli public. Israeli forces were surprised by the Arabs' strength and determination as their counterattack failed to dislodge the Egyptians from the Sinai. In the Sinai Campaign of 1956 and especially in the Six-Day War of 1967, Israeli forces had been able to overcome the Arabs quickly and with relatively few casualties. This time, however, Dayan was counseling an Israeli pullback to a line east of Suez, thinking that this would be easier to defend than the lines at the canal itself. He also counseled a significant retreat in the Golan. Dayan was overruled on both counts by Prime Minister Golda Meir and other members of the cabinet, all of whom were surprised at Dayan's apparent pessimism.

Dayan later wrote about the conflict:

> The Yom Kippur War was . . . not only a hard war to fight but also a hard atmosphere to fight in. We had to tackle mass forces equipped with large quantities of powerful armor, guns, and

surface-to-air missiles. . . . Each day, each hour, brought news of tragedy — husbands killed, sons killed, sons of relatives, friends, acquaintances, colleagues, neighbors in town and village. Our people [were] wholly given over to grief and anxiety for their men who had fallen, who were captive, or who were wounded.

Dayan led the Israeli armed forces as he had in previous conflicts. Helped by arms airlifted from the United States, Israel was able to turn the war around. In Sinai, Ariel Sharon led a dramatic crossing of the Suez Canal, thereby surrounding the Egyptian Third Army. On the Golan Heights, Israeli troops moved to within artillery range of Damascus, the Syrian capital. The fighting ended with a cease-fire on October 24 and the Israelis in these dominant positions. Disengagement talks conducted via dramatic shuttle diplomacy by U.S. secretary of state Henry Kissinger resulted in Israel's withdrawal to prewar lines by the middle of 1974. If he had chosen to, Dayan could have laid claim to an overwhelming military victory.

However, the context was different. The high death toll — some 2,400 lives — and the staggering cost — estimated at nearly $7.4 billion, about as much as Israel's projected gross national product for the year — shocked the Israelis. They worried that the Arabs had won an important boost in self-esteem and might be emboldened to engage in further violence, and they asked why Israel had been, as they saw it, so unprepared for the attack. They asked what Dayan, in particular, had been doing in the previous years that had led to Israel's weakened

Mourners gather at the grave sites of loved ones who died in the Yom Kippur War. Israel paid a high price — more than 2,000 Israeli lives — for what many considered the military's lack of preparedness. By the time a cease-fire agreement was reached, there were calls for Dayan's resignation.

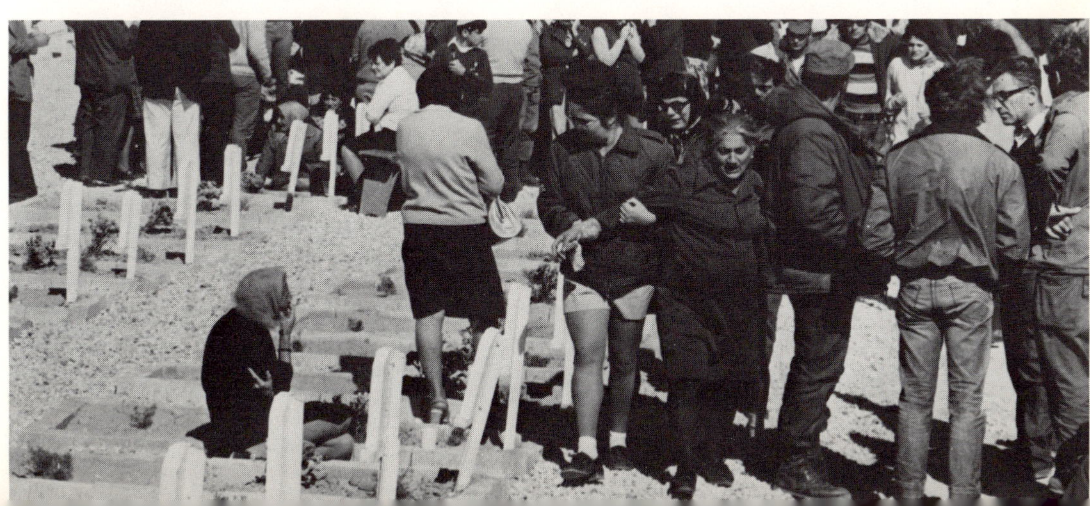

defense posture. They asked what they should do now that the image of the invincible Israeli had been undermined.

On December 31, 1973, Israelis were given a chance to render their verdict on the war at the polls. Many voters deserted the Labor party in large numbers for a new coalition known as the Likud (Hebrew for *unity*). The Likud featured two rising stars of Israeli politics — Ezer Weizmann, the sabra nephew of Chaim and the architect of Israel's air force, and Ariel Sharon, the only real hero to come out of the Yom Kippur War. Though Labor held on to power by winning 51 seats to the Likud's 39, the new coalition's showing was impressive and was an auger of changes to come in Israeli political life.

In November 1973, the Agranat Commission, named after Shimon Agranat, the president of Israel's supreme court, had been appointed to investigate the conduct of the war. An interim report delivered by the commission amidst a public furor over accountability exonerated Dayan from any wrongdoing and instead placed much of the blame on the chief of staff. The public was not mollified, thinking that Dayan, as minister of defense, and Golda Meir as well, had to share some responsibility for the grievous losses. Students, academics, writers, artists, and even soldiers called for Dayan's resignation.

Dayan later wrote of the controversy:

> A minister of defense needs the trust of the public. He is not just an impersonal director of a bureau. He, more than any other political officeholder, is responsible for decisions associated with war, with the killed and the wounded, with the prisoners and the missing, and with the bereaved families. The public may not share his views, but it is essential that they have faith in his integrity, dedication, understanding, and responsible approach to security affairs. I had the feeling that the public trust in me was being steadily undermined. On one occasion I passed some demonstrators as I was leaving a cabinet meeting and a young woman, probably a widow of a fallen soldier, cried out "Murderer!" It was a dagger in the heart.

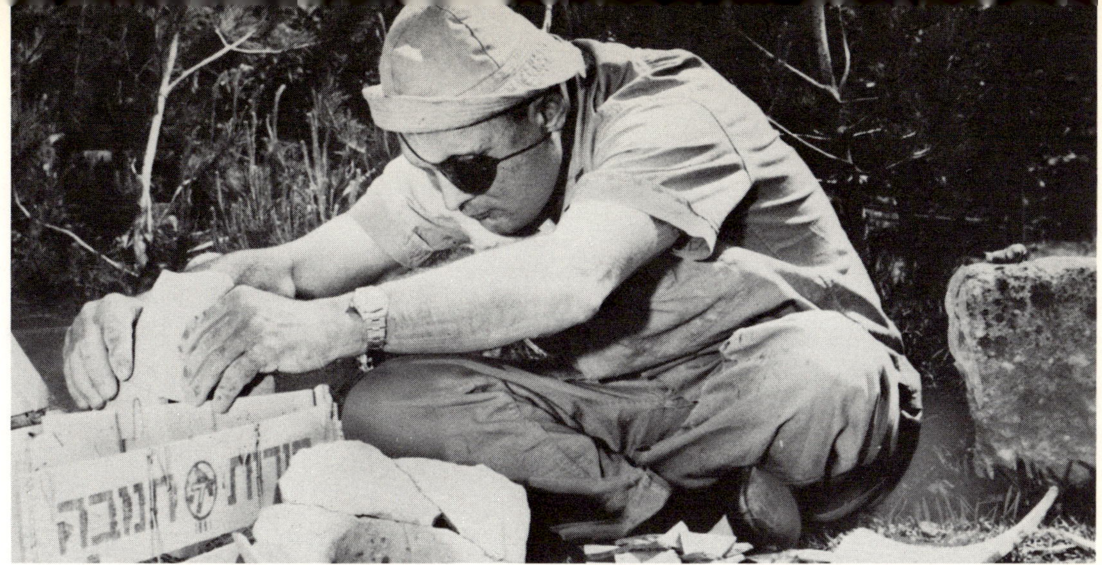

Still, Dayan did not resign, prompting further criticism that, while he was eager to claim credit for success, he was not so willing to own up to failure. Meir submitted her resignation, and Labor settled on Yitzhak Rabin as the new prime minister and Shimon Peres as the new minister of defense.

Dayan returned to civilian life to pursue his private passion — biblical archaeology. A respected amateur archeologist (though he often ignored laws and kept the artifacts he found for his private collection instead of placing them in the national archives), he wrote about archeology in the Holy Land in his book *Living with the Bible.* He wrote that he was looking for "the ancient Land of Israel. Everything that ancient Eretz-Israel was to those who lived here then; their way of life. You sometimes feel that you can literally enter their presence. They are dead to be sure. But you can enter the homes of silenced people and sometimes feel more than when you enter the homes of the living. I like to stick my head into a hole in which the people of Bnei Brak lived 6,000 years ago . . . to have a look at their kitchen, to finger the ashes left there from long ago, to feel the fingerprints which that ancient potter left on the vessel."

The Yom Kippur War and its aftermath brought Dayan to a low point in his life. But in a land whose soil boasts layer upon layer of history, in which civilizations have risen and fallen only to rise again, a pattern was obvious: Dayan sensed that he was not yet finished making history.

Dayan, who retired in 1974 to write his memoirs and to pursue his interest in biblical archaeology, works at an excavation site near Tel Aviv. His retirement proved to be only a brief respite from public life.

7

Breakthrough

As Israelis went to the polls on May 17, 1977, they were asked by those who stood for office to choose between distinct visions of the future. The Labor alignment, at that point the only government Israel had ever known, was in disarray, racked by scandals and thought by many to be running an unresponsive bureaucracy. Inflation had skyrocketed, and the economy required massive infusions of aid from the United States. Memories of the Yom Kippur War lingered, and many people resented the Labor establishment for its role in that conflict.

Still, no one was quite prepared for what happened next. In a shocking upset, Labor was turned out of office by the Likud, whose standard-bearer was Menachem Begin, the longtime opposition leader whom many considered a terrorist.

Begin had hired Ezer Weizmann to run his campaign. Weizmann succeeded in transforming Begin's image, as one writer put it, "from rambunctious rebel to solid statesman." First of all, there was no questioning his patriotism. Begin was also portrayed as an "incorruptible" leader, in obvious contrast to the Labor government politicians.

Egyptian president Anwar Sadat, U.S. president Jimmy Carter, and Israeli prime minister Menachem Begin (left to right) celebrate the signing of an Arab-Israeli peace treaty at the White House in 1979. The agreement was reached after 13 days of intense negotiation at Camp David, the presidential retreat in Maryland.

His long-standing position against giving up the occupied territories won him support from the country's religious elements, many of whom were moving into these areas. And his generally hawkish attitudes won him a large following from Jews who had fled to Israel from Arabic-speaking countries, primarily Morocco, Algeria, Egypt, Iraq, and Syria. These Jews are generally known as the Sephardim, whereas Jews of central or eastern European origin are known as Ashkenazim. The Ashkenazim were in the forefront of the Zionist movement and generally backed the Labor party. The Sephardim were discriminated against by the more sophisticated Ashkenazim in matters of employment, education, and housing. Begin had long been the champion of the Sephardim; his political party called itself the party of the "poor, the suffering, and the oppressed." The Sephardim also identified with Begin's ideas of Jewish strength and his hard-line stance toward the Arabs, under whose persecution they had lived for many years.

The Likud was thus able to win 43 seats to Labor's 32, and in June Begin was installed as prime minister, leading a 63-seat coalition government in the Knesset. Joining him to form this parliamentary majority were the religious parties and Moshe Dayan, who made a startling defection from Labor ranks to become Begin's foreign minister.

Such a move was without precedent in Israeli politics. It was made all the more dramatic by the stark differences that separated the Likud and Labor parties — differences in ideology and policy with roots going back to the earliest days of the Zionist movement. When Begin telephoned Dayan to make the offer, Dayan found himself in a quandary: "The inner struggle over whether to accept or refuse the appointment . . . was the toughest I had ever known. Abandoning my party and joining the government of our rival would mean a final break with my remaining Labor friends. . . . Would I find a common language with Begin and his associates in the government? True, I was closer to his views on political matters than I was to those of the Labor party leadership at that time; but I was not with him on all issues. And as for our social outlook, I was part of the very fiber of the socialist farm-settlement movement. How could I share collective responsibility in a Begin government when we shared no common basis in this social and economic sphere?"

Dayan's primary differences with Begin concerned the Arabs. Dayan did not believe in extending Israeli sovereignty to the territories occupied during the Six-Day War and sought assurances from Begin on this issue. He got them. Three days after Begin's momentous call Dayan accepted the job as foreign minister.

When Dayan's decision was made public, he was subjected to widespread disparagement by many Israelis. In the Knesset he was the focus of hostile looks and angry cries. In the mail he received angry letters criticizing him for turning his back on Labor Zionism and calling him an opportunist. Dayan, though accustomed to controversy, was not immune to such attacks. Still, for him, he felt, the major factor to consider was whether or not, as foreign minister, he could play a constructive role in seeking peace with Israel's Arab neighbors and the residents of the occupied territories. His answer was a definitive yes.

Jewish Sephardim arrive in Israel after a long journey from Morocco. In Israel the Sephardim, who are non-European Jews primarily from North Africa, encountered employment, education, and housing discrimination, which they considered lesser evils than the Arab persecution they had known in their native countries.

Begin, too, was in the eye of a storm. His accession to power was met with dismay abroad because of his image as an extremist. Nonetheless, Begin promised goodwill and said that a dramatic overture for peace would be made during his administration.

The overture came, but it was not made by Begin. On November 9, 1977, Egyptian president Anwar Sadat addressed his country's parliament: "Israel will be stunned to hear me tell you that I am ready to go to their home, to the Knesset itself, to argue with them, in order to prevent one Egyptian soldier from being wounded. Members of the People's Assembly, we have no time to waste." Sadat had on many occasions stated his willingness to go "to the ends of the earth" in search of peace; the Knesset element in this pronouncement was a new and important departure.

Begin's reply was given through an American intermediary, for Israel and Egypt were still formally at war and had no diplomatic relations. Begin invited Sadat to come to Jerusalem. "May I assure you, Mr. President," the message said, "that the parliament, the government, and the people of Israel will receive you with respect and cordiality." Thus was set in motion the historic face-to-face encounters that led to the first peace treaty between Israel and one of its Arab neighbors.

Just days after Sadat's historic address, his plane landed at Israel's Ben-Gurion Airport. Greeting Sadat were his enemies from the Sinai war four years earlier. To Golda Meir, he said, "Madame, I have been waiting to meet you for a long time." To Ariel Sharon, he said, "I wanted to catch you there." Sharon replied, "I'm glad to meet you here instead." To General Mordechai Gur, who warned the nation that Sadat might be using his visit as a ruse to start a war, he said, "I wasn't bluffing."

Sadat was greeted joyously wherever he went. Throughout his triumphant visit, during which he prayed at the el-Aksa Mosque and visited Yad Vashem, the Holocaust memorial and museum, Sadat delighted Israelis with his intelligence and candor. To most it was a dream come true, yet all

Israelis also knew that the trip and the forces it set in motion were loaded with risk.

Sadat's gamble lay primarily in his breaking with the Arab refusal to recognize Israel's right to exist. Many Arabs vehemently opposed Sadat's peace overtures. The Palestinians regarded Sadat's actions as a betrayal and continued to press their claims for a homeland. There was a real possibility that Sadat would be assassinated. He insisted that he was acting on behalf of all Arabs and that he was not trying to conclude a separate peace, as many of his critics charged. He promised to press the Arabs' case for Jerusalem and the occupied territories. The risk for Israel lay in being forced, for the sake of peace, to withdraw from the occupied territories.

The two leaders' addresses before the Knesset gave an indication of how difficult the approaching negotiations would be. Sadat's performance was impressive. In sincere tones he said the words Israelis had waited a very long time to hear from an Arab leader: "We agree to live with you in peace and justice. Israel has become an accomplished fact, recognized by the whole world and the superpowers. We welcome you to live among us in peace and security." Sadat then voiced the Arabs' demand that all lands occupied by Israel in 1967 be returned. The challenge for peace had been issued.

Anwar Sadat prays at the el-Aksa Mosque in Jerusalem in 1977. Although Sadat's trip to Israel was a mission of peace, many Arabs, and especially Palestinian Arabs, considered the Egyptian president's willingness to negotiate with the Israelis a betrayal.

Begin's response was less compelling. He restated many old positions, leading some people to fear that Sadat, for all his vision and trouble, would be going home "empty-handed." It was clear that Begin had found it hard to fashion a suitable reply to Sadat.

Moshe Dayan described later the alarm he had felt at this point: "I was deeply concerned about the price Egypt was determined to exact from us — total evacuation from Sinai; a commitment to withdraw completely from the West Bank and Golan; the rise of a Palestinian state. I sensed that there was a deep feeling behind these words; they were not mere lip-service. And I suspected that Israel would indeed be faced by the grim alternative of having to make heavy concessions or achieving no peace treaty with Egypt."

December was marked by a flurry of diplomatic activity. Days after Sadat returned to Cairo, he asked that Dayan make a secret trip to Morocco to speak with that country's King Hassan, who has often played the role of mediator in the Middle East, and with Dr. Hassan Tuhami, a high-ranking Egyptian emissary. The discussions featured a frank airing of positions but did not lead to much progress. Dayan left thinking that a United States role in the peace process was necessary. That process was to be made that much more difficult by subsequent developments in Tripoli, Libya, where the other Arab states, meeting in conference, declared an economic and diplomatic boycott of Egypt.

Late that month, Begin, Dayan, and Ezer Weizmann visited the Egyptian city of Ismailia. The trip
was intended, at least in part, to reciprocate the
hospitality Israel had shown for Sadat. To Dayan,
the contrast in this regard was striking:

> The town of Ismailia had a festive air, with
> banners and bunting and arches of honor at
> the main crossroads, and Egyptian flags flut-
> tering from the rooftops above the swept
> streets. Yet I was troubled in spirit. It began
> with our arrival at the airport. When Sadat
> came to Israel he was received with the full
> panoply of accustomed protocol. Though I have
> already indicated my own attitude to pomp and
> ceremony, there are occasions when they carry
> political implications — and certainly so when
> they are absent. Our reception at the Ismailia
> airport was marked by studied casualness —
> no guard of honor, no Israeli flags, no national
> anthems. Even in the city itself, the streamers
> at the crossroads and giant posters in the
> streets bore slogans praising "Sadat, bringer
> of peace." There was no mention of Begin and
> not a single welcoming sign.

Algerian president Houari Boumédienne, Palestine Liberation Organization leader Yasir Arafat, Iraqi leader Tahe Yasin Ramsdan, and Libya's Muammar el-Qaddafi (left to right) arrive in Tripoli, Libya, for a conference of Arab leaders opposed to Sadat's visit to Israel. At the conference, they agreed to an economic and diplomatic boycott of Egypt.

Here, too, there was a sincere exchange over the two countries' relative positions, but the gap remained wide, and some tension could even be felt. Committees were formed to study the issues as a way of keeping some momentum going.

During the next several months, it was Begin who was perceived, at least by the foreign press, as the intransigent "obstacle" to peace for not being more flexible about the occupied territories. Soon the excitement and optimism that had followed Sadat's visit began to give way to doubt. In the end, it was the intensive involvement of U.S. president Jimmy Carter that salvaged the last remains of Egyptian-Israeli goodwill and paved the way for a historic peace treaty.

Carter, elected in 1976, had on many occasions voiced his desire to help bring about a comprehensive peace settlement in the Middle East. Some of his pronouncements, however, especially those calling for a Palestinian homeland and for Israeli flexibility over the West Bank and Gaza, had led many Israelis to consider him too close to the Arab camp. In particular, they feared that because America was Israel's most important foreign ally, Israel would be forced to accept an agreement that would not take into account the country's security needs.

Carter and Begin had established a cordial relationship: Carter had stressed his continued willingness to supply Israel with generous military and economic aid. Still, he had found reason to write in his diary in the spring of 1978, "My guess is that he [Begin] will not take the necessary steps to bring peace to Israel."

In January, Carter journeyed to the Egyptian city of Aswan to try and break through the increasing divide that was developing between Egypt and Israel. Just two weeks later, however, an Egyptian delegation to Israel abruptly packed its bags and left after Begin had interjected a political note to evening dinner festivities that were supposed to be devoid of such pronouncements. Begin had also inadvertently offended one of the Egyptian diplomats by calling him "young man." Dayan felt that the Egyptian behavior had also been arrogant.

A further blow to the talks was delivered in March, when Palestinian terrorists commandeered a bus along the Haifa–Tel Aviv highway; 35 Israelis were killed and 71 wounded in the incident. Israel and Dayan retaliated with an extensive invasion of southern Lebanon to rid that area of Palestinian guerrilla bases that had been set up there. (Lebanon's civil war, which started in 1975, had created a power vacuum that allowed Palestinian guerrillas to operate freely in much of the country.) Many people, Dayan included, saw Israel as justified in its response. But the so-called Litani Operation — named after the Litani River, which divides southern and northern Lebanon — also disrupted the lives of many Lebanese civilians (who themselves disliked the Palestinian presence), further inflaming the Arabs. As the talks with Egypt continued to show no progress, Sadat's position in the Arab world grew more grave.

In July the parties met at Leeds Castle in England for their first face-to-face talks in six months. Here, too, they remained far apart regarding central issues. Though U.S. secretary of state Cyrus Vance subsequently traveled to the Middle East to keep the dialogue from lapsing, it was clear that something dramatic was needed. So, Carter went out on an unprecedented diplomatic limb by bringing Begin, Sadat, and their respective negotiating teams to the Camp David presidential retreat in Maryland for several days of talks.

The Camp David summit meeting started on September 5 and ended on September 17. Carter reported that Sadat and Begin each drove a hard bargain. "All restraint was gone," he wrote. "Their faces were flushed and the niceties of diplomatic language and protocol were stripped away. They had

almost forgotten that I was there." At one point
Carter had to block the door of the cabin to keep a
frustrated Sadat from walking out on the talks. And
as the days wound down it appeared as if the conference would end with both delegations issuing
statements explaining why they could not agree to
the other's terms. Finally, with the creative input of
presidential aides and a painstaking attention to
detail on the part of Carter, formulas were reached,
appropriate language was agreed upon, and the
foundations for peace were laid. Sadat and Begin,
who had last seen each other on day three of the
talks, came together on day thirteen and promised
to conclude a treaty within three months.

Commentators say that it was also Dayan who
came up with the compromises that kept the Camp
David negotiations moving forward. He and Sadat
were able to work together despite the lack of personal warmth between them. Likewise, he and
Carter found common ground even though Carter
was very demanding on Israeli positions. And, cru-
cially, Dayan had the complete trust of Begin, who
knew that Dayan, of all people, would never agree
to anything that would risk Israel's security.
Through all of it Dayan put incredible strain upon
his eye, so much so that he finally had to have aides
read to him.

The Camp David talks produced two documents,
one that was to serve as the framework for an overall
Middle East peace and another that was to be the
framework for a separate Egypt-Israel peace treaty.
The happy conclusion had been hard in coming:
Carter said after the exhausting negotiations that
no one had expected "13 intense and discouraging
days, with success in prospect only during the final
hours."

Back in Israel, the debate over the agreements was
furious. Some people thought Begin had made too
many concessions. Dayan, ever the realist, added
his voice to the Knesset debate about the historic
peace:

> The Egypt-Israel peace treaty, I told the House,
> was not a pastoral idyll full of sweetness and
> sunshine and repose in lush meadows. It was

not the fulfillment of Isaiah's end-of-days vision when swords would be beaten into ploughshares, and nation would not lift up sword against nation any more. . . . This was a realistic peace treaty, set in the context of current realities, and designed to bring about relations between two neighboring countries, Egypt and Israel, as normal as those between any other two countries in the world.

The Knesset approved the accords. In October 1978, Begin and Sadat were awarded the Nobel Peace Prize.

The two then hardened their positions. Begin accelerated settlement on the West Bank in the apparent hope that, come the day when withdrawal was to occur, these "facts on the ground" might prevent the Israeli departure. He also defined more narrowly what he meant by the "autonomy" the Camp David accords would grant to the Palestinians living under Israeli rule. Sadat, for his part, sought to link the overall accords more closely with the fate of the Palestinians, in reaction to intensive Arab opposition to the entire process and their charge that he had sold out the Palestinian cause. By March 1, Begin stated that the peace talks were "in a state of deep crisis."

Carter embarked on a week of shuttle diplomacy between Cairo and Jerusalem. As with the talks at Camp David, his efforts frequently came close to failure. But on March 13 he secured final guarantees from Begin and Sadat, and two weeks later they were in Washington together, where they signed the pact amid great fanfare. (Carter signed the document as a witness.)

Several thousand people were crowded onto the White House lawn to watch the historic ceremony, and a worldwide audience estimated at 100 million people saw the event on television.

Speaking to the excited onlookers, Begin quoted the famous words of the prophet Isaiah:

> And they shall beat their swords into plowshares,
> And their spears into pruning hooks;
> Nation shall not lift up sword against nation,
> Neither shall they learn war anymore.

He went on to say, "Despite the tragedies and disappointments of the past, we must never forsake that vision, that human dream, that unshakable faith."

Coincidentally, Carter and Sadat used the very same Old Testament words in their speeches. Sadat's remarks included an eloquent pronouncement of his own: "Let there be no more war or bloodshed between Arabs and Israelis. Let there be no more suffering or denial of rights. Let there be no more despair or loss of faith. Let no mother lament the loss of her child. Let no young man waste his life on a conflict from which no one benefits."

The most dramatic moment of the ceremony occurred after the three leaders had signed the document. (Three copies of the treaty had been prepared — one in English, one in Arabic, and one in Hebrew.) Rising to their feet, the three peacemakers joined hands in a three-way handshake and smiled broadly. Carter said to his two guests: "I'm so proud of you." The pact was sealed.

The treaty provided for a three-stage Israeli withdrawal from the Sinai Peninsula. UN peacekeeping forces would be stationed along the Israel-Egypt border. Israeli ships would be free to pass through the Suez Canal, the Strait of Tiran, and the Gulf of Aqaba, and Israel would have the right to purchase oil, under normal commercial terms, from the Sinai fields. Full diplomatic relations and economic and cultural ties between the two nations were established. In addition, a month after the treaty was ratified by the two countries' parliaments, negotiations were to begin on Palestinian autonomy in the West Bank and Gaza. Upon the successful completion of these talks, Israeli rule in these territories was to end.

Unaffected by the Camp David treaty was the status of Jerusalem and the Golan Heights, and trouble was sure to accompany any Israeli retreat from the West Bank. But these were secondary considerations, at least for the moment. What most observers at the time focused on was that the rift between Egypt and Israel had been closed. Thirty years of war were over.

8

The Final Battles

It is said often about the Middle East that peace, like war, has to be waged. Dayan, Carter, Sadat, and Begin harbored no illusions that simply signing a piece of paper meant peace had been achieved. Indeed, the immediate effect of the Camp David treaty was not peace but turmoil.

Angered that Sadat had chosen to make peace with Israel, Arab nations severed diplomatic and economic ties with Egypt. Of all Arab countries, Egypt is the most populated and most heavily armed Arab nation and was traditionally the Arab world's chief representative on the international stage. Egypt's neighbors felt they were being betrayed by Sadat.

Begin caused Egypt further anxiety. He clarified his position on the treaty, asserting that Jerusalem would never again be a divided city, that a Palestinian state would never be established on the West Bank, and that Israel would never return to its pre-1967 borders. As Begin's views on these issues became increasingly uncompromising, Dayan became alienated. Finally, in October 1979, Dayan decided he could no longer serve Begin in good faith:

The passage of thousands of years has not erased the traces of the ancient past.
—MOSHE DAYAN

Dayan resigned his post in the Begin government in October 1979. He and the prime minister were unable to reconcile their conflicting views on the occupied territories and Israel's obligations under the Camp David accords.

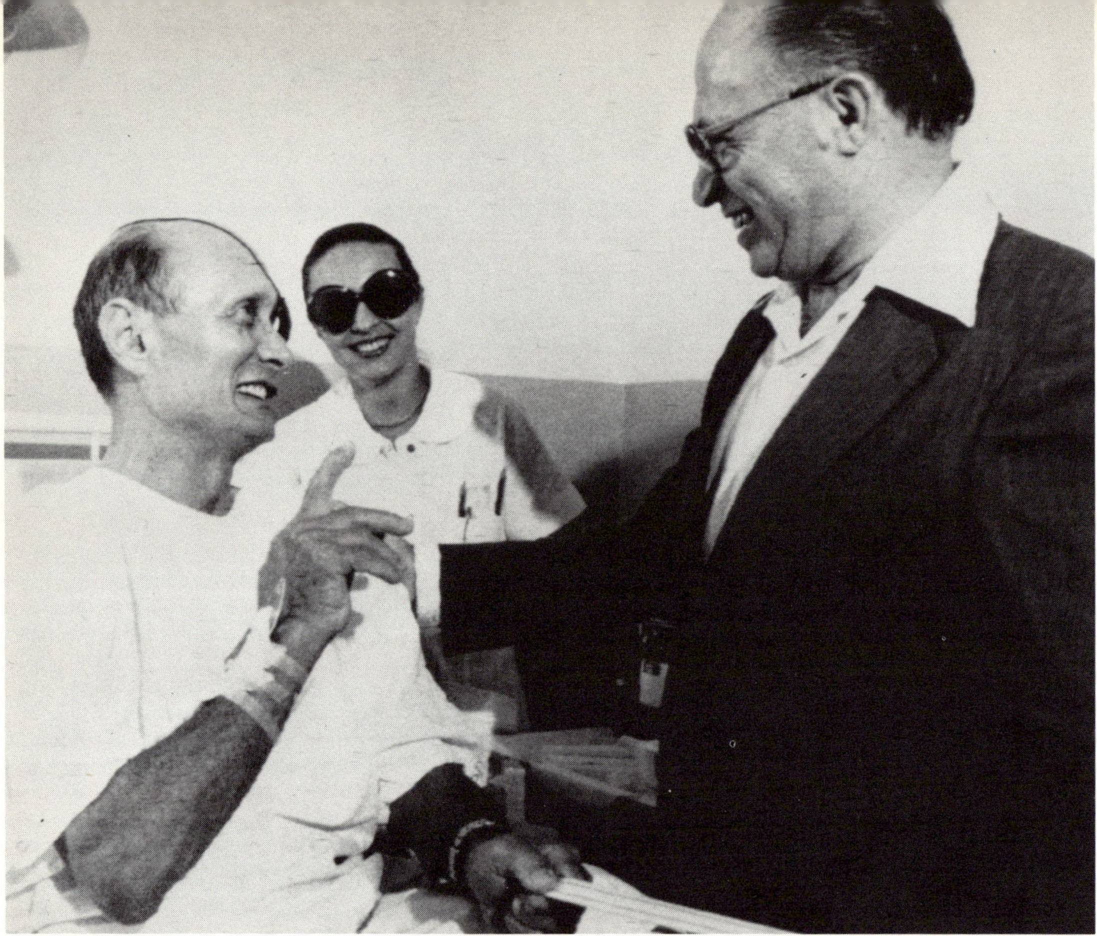

Begin visits Dayan in a Tel Aviv hospital in June 1974, when Dayan discovered he had colon cancer. Intestinal surgery was performed days after he received the diagnosis, and he was released from the hospital with an excellent prognosis.

I had . . . had enough of the continued carping by my ministerial colleague, who always thought I was exceeding my authority and was too ready to compromise and give in to the Egyptians and the Americans. . . . The gap between our respective approaches toward the future of the Arabs in Judea, Samaria, and the Gaza District was too wide to bridge. Begin and his party wanted these territories to be under Israeli sovereignty, though I doubted whether they had crystallized their views on what would be the status of the Arab inhabitants. From statements made by Begin, I gathered he was prepared to grant them autonomy within the framework of the State of Israel. I, on the other hand, did not believe that Israeli sovereignty could be imposed on these Arabs against their will. Moreover, even if all or some of them requested it, a government structure was required that ensured that the Arab element would not deprive Israel of her distinctive Jewish character.

This political crisis came on the heels of a personal crisis Dayan had faced earlier in the year. In June he was found to have cancer of the colon. He was operated on within days of the diagnosis, and later pronounced healthy, save for some minor irregularities. The fortitude he displayed through this ordeal recalls the 18 hours of suffering he endured after being shot in the eye nearly 40 years earlier. But Dayan, a fearless soldier, was no stranger to death.

"There have been moments in my life which I had good reason to believe were my last, and I know that the thought did not worry me," he wrote. "Over the years, anxiety about mortality ceased to occupy any part of my consciousness. The prospect of death was of no interest to me, and had no effect on my way of life. The guiding forces of that way of life were yearning, ambition and faith." Just three weeks after the operation, Dayan was back at work.

Dayan suffered a fatal heart attack on October 16, 1981. Rahel Dayan attends the funeral of her husband at Nahalal. His body was finally laid to rest on the Galilee farm collective where he spent his childhood.

Dayan's last venture in active politics came in 1981 with his founding of a new political party, Telem. Among other things, Telem advocated a unilateral Israeli military withdrawal from the West Bank and Gaza Strip. Dayan was still hoping to influence Israeli policy on the issue closest to his heart — relations with the Arabs. But this time it was not to be. In June elections, Telem won only two seats; meanwhile, Begin was returned to power in the closest election in Israel's history.

On October 16, Dayan was taken to Tel Hashomer Hospital in Tel Aviv, after suffering chest pains the night before. (Dayan had a history of heart trouble.) He had suffered a heart attack. Yael Dayan, called to the hospital by Rahel, said her father's face at this point "had the intensity of an angry fighter unable to grasp the dreadful thing that was happening to him." She also described what he looked like hours later, after he lost consciousness and doctors were unable to revive him: "I have seen many dead faces. Tranquil or accepting, amazed or tor-

Two Palestinian boys bolster a burning barricade at the southern entrance to the city of Gaza, on the Gaza Strip, in 1987. In Gaza and throughout the occupied territories violence is a way of life: Reports of clashes between local Palestinians and Israeli soldiers stationed there have become increasingly prevalent in the 1980s.

tured, childish or wrinkled. My father's conveyed angry frustration, as if he didn't mean it to happen quite then, and for the first time ever was caught unaware, deprived of the last word. Those things unsaid and unaccomplished hovered there, almost palpable. This furious aura has haunted me ever since."

Ten days earlier, Anwar Sadat had been assassinated by Muslim fundamentalists opposed to his efforts at making peace with Israel and his dealings with the United States and other Western countries. Israel's withdrawal from the Sinai was completed on April 25, 1982. But as the negotiations over Palestinian autonomy failed to progress, and with Egypt in isolation and Israel unwilling to budge over the occupied territories, the two countries settled into what has come to be known as the cold peace. The borders remain open, flags fly in the two capitals, but there is only a smattering of contact.

The situation in the occupied West Bank and Gaza Strip has grown more complex and volatile in the years since Dayan's death, and the future does not look promising. There is violence in the region daily as Palestinians resist Israeli occupation and

Palestine Liberation Organization leader Yasir Arafat. Since being elected chairman of the organization in 1969, Arafat has been its principal representative, articulating its goals and defending the rights of the Palestinian Arabs who live in the occupied territories.

Israeli soldiers assert a strong presence. Israel has been severely criticized by the international community for the violent methods its military has used to stifle civilian Arab resistance and by Amnesty International for alleged human rights violations such as imprisonment without trial, prisoner abuse, and press censorship. Inhabitants of the occupied territories are not considered citizens and are denied the right to vote; political parties are banned.

Meanwhile, the large and very powerful Palestine Liberation Organization (PLO), a group that seeks, often by the use of violent means, to establish an independent Palestinian state, in 1987 announced its intention to escalate its armed struggle. The PLO's chief spokesperson, Yasir Arafat, has proposed a plan for a Palestinian state coexistent with Israel, but its implementation would require Israel to relinquish control of the occupied territories, something it shows no sign of being willing to do.

Arafat warns that by the year 2000, at the current growth rate, half of Israel's population (including the occupied territories) could be Arabs and soon after Arabs may outnumber Israel's Jews. This, he points out, could make Israel a state in which a ruling minority systematically oppresses a majority of its inhabitants, an arrangement clearly inconsistent with Israel's democratic principles.

Many believe that the fate of the entire Middle East, and perhaps the world, depends on that of the Israeli occupied territories. The situation seems to cry out for Dayan's deep understanding of the Arabs and his knowledge of what constitutes security for the Jews. But Dayan is dead, buried at Nahalal. During his life he made an indelible mark on the Holy Land.

Dayan may have written his own epitaph in a 1980 newspaper interview: "I just want to be buried at Nahalal in the family cemetery on the hill where the children play. No speeches, no pictures, no honors. I never accepted honorary titles in life; I don't want them in death. What do you want to be an honorary doctor for? Either you're a doctor or you're not. Either you're alive or you're not. That's all."

Moshe Dayan chats with an Israeli Arab in the late 1970s. As resentment and violence in the occupied territories has intensified, the need for someone with Dayan's ability to negotiate with Arab leaders has grown proportionately. Moshe Dayan will be remembered not only as a great man of arms but also as a man of reason.

Further Reading

Amdur, Richard. *Chaim Weizmann.* New York: Chelsea House, 1988.

———. *Menachem Begin.* New York: Chelsea House, 1987.

Beit-Hallahmi, Benjamin. *The Israeli Connection.* New York: Pantheon, 1987.

Chomsky, Noam. *Peace in the Middle East?* New York: Pantheon, 1974.

Dayan, Moshe. *Breakthrough: A Personal Account of the Egypt-Israel Peace Negotiations.* London: Weidenfeld & Nicolson, 1981.

———. *Diary of the Sinai Campaign.* New York: Harper & Row, 1966.

———. *Living with the Bible.* New York: Morrow, 1978.

———. *Story of My Life.* New York: Morrow, 1976.

Dayan, Ruth, and Helga Dudman. *And Perhaps . . . The Story of Ruth Dayan.* New York: Harcourt Brace Jovanovich, 1973.

Dayan, Yael. *My Father, His Daughter.* New York: Farrar, Straus & Giroux, 1985.

Elon, Amos. *The Israelis: Founders and Sons.* New York: Holt, Rinehart, and Winston, 1971.

Laqueur, Walter. *A History of Zionism.* New York: Holt, Rinehart, and Winston, 1976.

Lau-Lavie, Naphtalie. *Moshe Dayan: A Biography.* London: Vallentine, Mitchell, 1968.

Sachar, Howard M. *A History of Israel.* New York: Knopf, 1976.

Teveth, Shabtai. *Moshe Dayan: The Soldier, the Man, the Legend.* Boston: Houghton Mifflin, 1972.

Vail, John J. *David Ben-Gurion.* New York: Chelsea House, 1987.

Chronology

May 4, 1915	Moshe Dayan is born at Degania in Galilee.
1917	Great Britain issues the Balfour Declaration.
1929	Dayan joins the Haganah.
1935	Marries Ruth Shwarz.
1937	Joins the Jewish Settlement Police, a British-Israeli commando unit.
1939	Imprisoned for illegal arms possession; the British white paper issued.
1941	Released from prison.
1939–45	World War II; Dayan joins the British army and fights in Lebanon and Syria in 1941; loses an eye in battle.
1947	Britain gives up its mandate in Palestine; UN votes for partition of the region.
May 14, 1948	State of Israel is established.
1948–49	Israel's War of Independence; Dayan becomes commander of Jerusalem, with the rank of lieutenant colonel, then earns the rank of major general and leads Southern Command.
1952	Dayan becomes head of Northern Command.
1953	Appointed chief of staff.
1956	Oversees the capture of the Sinai Peninsula.
1959	Becomes minister of agriculture.
1964	Resigns and returns to private life.
1967	Returns to public life; becomes minister of defense. In the Six-Day War, Dayan spearheads Israel's capture of the Golan Heights, the West Bank of the Jordan River, and East Jerusalem.
1971	Divorces Ruth Dayan at her request.
1973	Yom Kippur War.
1974	Dayan resigns to write his memoirs and to pursue interest in archaeology.
1977	Named foreign minister by newly elected prime minister Menachem Begin. Egyptian president Anwar Sadat visits Jerusalem.
1979	The Camp David Peace Treaty signed; Dayan resigns from the Begin government.
1981	Telem, the political party Dayan had formed, wins only two seats in the elections that return Begin to power.
Oct. 16, 1981	Dayan dies of a heart attack.

Richard Amdur is a New York based writer and editor with a continuing interest in the history of Israel, where he spent more than a year living and working on a kibbutz. He is the author of *Chaim Weizmann* and *Menachem Begin* in the Chelsea House series WORLD LEADERS—PAST & PRESENT, and his articles have appeared in the *New York Times*, *Psychology Today*, and *Cosmopolitan* magazine, among other publications.

Arthur M. Schlesinger, jr., taught history at Harvard for many years and is currently Albert Schweitzer Professor of the Humanities at City University of New York. He is the author of numerous highly praised works in American history and has twice been awarded the Pulitzer Prize. He served in the White House as special assistant to Presidents Kennedy and Johnson.

PICTURE CREDITS